The Fight for
English

The Fight for
English

~

HOW LANGUAGE PUNDITS ATE,
SHOT, AND LEFT

David Crystal

OXFORD
UNIVERSITY PRESS

OXFORD
UNIVERSITY PRESS
Great Clarendon Street, Oxford ox2 6DP
Oxford University Press is a department of the University of Oxford.
It furthers the University's objective of excellence in research, scholarship,
and education by publishing worldwide in

Oxford New York
Auckland Cape Town Dar es Salaam Hong Kong Karachi
Kuala Lumpur Madrid Melbourne Mexico City Nairobi
New Delhi Shanghai Taipei Toronto

With offices in
Argentina Austria Brazil Chile Czech Republic France Greece
Guatemala Hungary Italy Japan Poland Portugal Singapore
South Korea Switzerland Thailand Turkey Ukraine Vietnam

Oxford is a registered trade mark of Oxford University Press
in the UK and in certain other countries

Published in the United States
by Oxford University Press Inc., New York

First published 2006

British Library Cataloguing in Publication Data
Data available

Library of Congress Cataloging in Publication Data
Data available

Typeset by Cepha Imaging Pvt Ltd., Bangalore, India
Printed in Great Britain
by Clays Ltd, Bungay, Suffolk

ISBN 978-0-19-920764-0

Contents

Contents

Prologue

U NIMAGINABLE millions have bought Lynne Truss's book *Eats, Shoots and Leaves*. It was the publishing success story of the new millennium. Eat your heart out, Harry Potter. Here comes punctuation.

I have to admit to being completely taken aback. The book originated as a Radio 4 series of four programmes called 'Cutting a Dash'. I was a consultant for that series, and one of Lynne's contributors. We got on fine. I thought her approach was delightful, the right blend of serious interest and quirky thinking. Punctuation had never been a sexy subject, ever. If anything was going to make it so, I thought, this series would be it.

But a book? Never. After the interview, we were reflecting on the public interest—or rather, lack of it—in the subject. Write a book on punctuation? Remembering Eric Partridge's undersold guide, and a host of other long-neglected accounts that I have on my shelves, I made the stupidest remark of my life. 'I wouldn't bother. Books on punctuation never sell!'

So what do I know? I still have no clear idea why that book has done so well. Why did people buy it? What did they hope they would get out of it? Did they actually read it? What is it that makes people think that a book on punctuation will somehow solve their imagined language problems?

And after they have read it, do they feel any better? These are some of the questions I want to answer in this book.

Having said that, my book isn't especially about *Eats, Shoots and Leaves*, but rather about the whole genre of books which that book represents. Manuals of English usage have sold well for generations, and they all make the same claims. The curious thing is that the same issues that bug people now were bugging them 250 years ago. Life and language have moved on, but still people worry. Millions feel linguistically inferior. And their inferiority complex is reinforced by the muggle who stares out at us from many a newspaper advertisement: Are You Shamed By Your Mistakes In English? Deep down, everyone who has bought Lynne Truss's book—and millions more who haven't—thinks, 'Yes.'

How has all this happened? How have we been made to feel so ashamed of our own language? Is it possible to restore our linguistic self-confidence, after it has received such a battering? And, the most important question of all, how should we deal with the disturbing note that is creeping into contemporary debate on the subject? *Eats, Shoots and Leaves* has a subtitle: the 'zero tolerance' approach to punctuation. Zero tolerance? That is the language of crime prevention and political extremism. Are we really comfortable with the recommendation that we should all become linguistic fundamentalists? Lynne Truss seems to have fallen into bad company.

Or is it all, as one American reviewer of her book put it, a hoax? This opinion is about. In February 2006, a *Sunday Times* diarist, puzzled by my views on the matter, as briefly expressed in a chapter of my *How Language Works*, was unequivocal. The whole thing is a joke, and there must be something wrong with me if I can't see it. Well, the history of ideas—let alone Lynne Truss's subsequent interviews and the markedly unfunny harangues I regularly get from language pedants—suggests that it is no joke. Her book should not be summarily dismissed in this way.

I think it has to be taken seriously—in good humour, but seriously. I am indeed unhappy about the trend represented by *Eats, Shoots and Leaves*, and think we should resist it. But the first thing is to understand it. When did English usage start to become an issue? When did it become a Big Issue? Why do people feel so strongly about it? There is a lot that is good in the Trussian type of approach. Can we extract the good bits and jettison what is bad?

This is the story of the fight for English usage—the story of a group of people who tried to shape the language in their own image but, generation after generation, failed. They looked at the language around them, and didn't like what they saw. 'Fight' is not my metaphor, but theirs. 'We must fight to preserve the tongue that Shakespeare spoke,' said one newspaper headline, years ago. These crusaders devoured grammars, exploded in fury, fought long and hard, and then all but a few departed the field. To coin a phrase: they ate, shot, and left.

But not without some last-ditch skirmishes. There are still those who see themselves as defenders of the linguistic faith, and perhaps there always will be. And there is still an avid market for their books, as the Truss phenomenon demonstrates. So what is it that keeps the issue alive? And is it healthy? Some people will be surprised to learn that my answer to this last question is that it can be—but only if we step back from fundamentalism and adopt a more rational linguistic perspective.

My book is organized along broadly historical lines. I begin at the end of the Old English period, in the eleventh century, and trace the way questions of English usage, and associated attitudes, manifested themselves thereafter. The first eleven chapters take the story up to the eighteenth century, when there was a huge shift in the way people thought about usage. These chapters do not give a comprehensive account of the history of the language—that would be to rewrite my *Stories of English*—but rather present a selection of points which illustrate the way the attitudes we recognize today were being formed.

From Chapter 12 on, I depart from a purely chronological account, and begin to present the story of usage in terms of the main themes which people recognize today—notably grammar, punctuation, spelling, and pronunciation. I maintain a steady course towards the twenty-first century, throughout these later chapters, but I do pause at intervals to explore the nature of the issues that attract particular controversy. Then, in the final four chapters, I focus on the factors which have shaped the educational situation we see today, and take a view on where we are heading.

We have been through some hard times of late, with a number of reports claiming that school-leavers' linguistic abilities are not living up to expectations. There is a fresh educational focus on language now which indicates the arrival of a new era. In my last chapter, accordingly, I am cautiously optimistic.

D.C.

Regulations

I

Beginnings

WHO was the first person ever to worry about English usage? Maybe it was a topic which preoccupied Beowulf and his friends in the Germanic beer-halls, but all the evidence suggests that the talk there was less about how to deal with grammar than how to deal with Grendel. The only clauses that Beowulf had to deal with were at the end of that half-human monster's fingers.

In the monasteries, though, things were rather different. The Beowulf story is preserved in a manuscript which dates from around the year 1000. And not long after, we find the first recorded example of a conversation in English, in the *Colloquium*—or 'Colloquy'—of Abbot Ælfric (pronounced al-fritch) of Eynsham. Buried within this document is the first brief mention in the English language of a concern to 'get things right'.

Ælfric was born about 955 and died about 1020. He was educated in the Benedictine monastery at Winchester, and became a teacher at the abbey of Cernel—now Cerne Abbas—in Dorset. Then in 1005 he was appointed abbot of the newly founded monastery at Eynsham, near Oxford. A translator of the Bible and the author of many homilies in Old English, he also wrote a Latin grammar—and, as a result, came to be known as Ælfric the Grammarian.

English at the time was still emerging as a language of literature. In the ninth century, King Alfred had eloquently pleaded for more works to be written in English and to be translated into English, and bemoaned the fact that there were so few people capable of doing such work. A century on, things had much improved, but the classical language was still the dominant voice of debate. Ælfric wrote his Colloquy in Latin, and it was one of his students who later turned it into English, adding tiny glosses above the Latin words in a manuscript.

Anyone studying Latin—as all educated people did, in those days—would know that the 'art' of effective speaking and writing had been a recurrent theme of Roman authors a thousand years before. Questions of rhetoric and style had been thoroughly discussed by Aristotle, Cicero, Longinus, and many others, and their notion that some styles of expression were elegant and acceptable while others were not was taken as gospel. Those authors, moreover, didn't just write about style: they demonstrated it in their own writing. Latin presented everyone with a series of undisputed literary classics, whose linguistic sophistication—it was universally believed—could not be surpassed. Other languages would do very well, it was felt, if they could only live up to the standards illustrated by Latin.

So when we read the following lines in the Colloquy, we can understand them as having a double application. They are about Latin, certainly, but they have serious implications for anyone writing in English. The dialogue begins: 'Nos pueri rogamus te magister… We cildra biddaþ þe, lareow…'

> We boys ask you, master, that you teach us to speak Latin correctly, because we are ignorant and we speak ungrammatically.

The master asks, 'What do you want to speak?' To which the boys reply:

> What do we care what we speak, as long as the speech is correct and useful, not foolish or base?!

And just in case such boys might be having him on, the master adds: 'Are you ready to be beaten while you learn?' Their reply does strain credulity somewhat—but then, the writer is the teacher, not the students:

> We would rather be beaten for our teaching than not to know it.

There we have it: 'as long as the speech is correct'. In the Old English, 'buton hit riht spræc sy'. In the Latin original, 'nisi recta locutio sit'. And how would everyone have decided whether their language was 'riht'? By looking in their Latin grammar. That was where the rules of the language—rules of spelling, pronunciation, word formation, and sentence construction—were laid down. Ælfric would doubtless have used his own grammar—that is what teachers who have written a book always do—but his text was just the latest in a long line of Latin grammars stretching back over a thousand years. There could have been no doubt in anyone's mind

as to what 'correct Latin' was. The grammars and dictionaries told you. And the grammarians and lexicographers
based their rules on the best language of the best authors—
people like Cicero, Livy, Horace, and Virgil. The task was to
make sure you followed those rules scrupulously. The birch
was never far away, if you didn't.

In Anglo-Saxon times, the analogous concept of a 'correct
English' would have made no sense, because there was no
canon of great literature to provide the raw material for
grammars and dictionaries. Nor, in any case, were there
any grammarians and lexicographers. The nearest we get
are the glossators—scribes who glossed lists of Latin words
in Old English. They provide us with some of the earliest
samples of the English language. But there was nothing
remotely resembling what we would today understand as
a grammar and a dictionary. Such enterprises—and the
associated beatings—were 600 years in the future.

Even if, as a thought experiment, we imagine modern
grammarians back in Anglo-Saxon times, it would not be
possible for them to come up with a text which would say
what 'correct usage' was. The Angles, Saxons, and Jutes who
brought English to Britain in the fifth century spoke different Germanic dialects, and these quickly spread throughout the country. The Old English texts show that there
were five main dialect areas in England, each with its own
local pronunciation, grammar, and vocabulary. We can see
the differences especially in the spellings. Here is the opening
line of the Lord's Prayer ('Our father who art in heaven'), as
written down, in texts dating from the 10th–11th centuries,

in three of these areas: the north-east, east midlands, and south.

North: fader urer ðu art in heofnu
Midlands: feder ure þu eart in heofenum
South: fæder ure þu þe eart on heofonum

With such widespread diversity, who would ever be able to say whether the version used by the monks up in Jarrow was 'more correct' than those used in Lincoln or Winchester? Unlike the situation in Latin, there was no one dialect recognized as the one to be used by educated English-users everywhere. There was no 'standard' English.

There *nearly* was. As the literature of the Anglo-Saxon period grew in range and quantity, one of these dialects—the one based in the south, at Winchester in Wessex—did develop a special status. King Alfred's political, cultural, and linguistic initiatives gave that dialect—West Saxon, as it later came to be called—a prestige which made it influential well beyond the borders of his kingdom. More and more manuscripts came to be written in it. Monks from as far away as Dorset and Worcestershire started to write in a West Saxon way. A standard was slowly appearing. A notion of correct usage was beginning to emerge. You can see it in such writers as Ælfric, who warns his copyists to avoid making mistakes:

Now I desire and beseech, in God's name, if anyone will transcribe this book, that he carefully correct it by the copy, lest we be blamed through careless writers. He does great evil who writes carelessly, unless he correct it. It is as though he turn true doctrine into false error.

Ælfric was talking about the content, primarily, but his point applied just as much to the language. Notions such as 'careless' and 'error' anticipate later attitudes.

If matters had been allowed to take their course, a powerful standard language might soon have emerged, along with an associated snobbery, and a grammar of 'correct' Old English might well have been written in the early Middle Ages. But matters did not follow the expected course. William the Conqueror saw to that.

2

Complications

THE arrival of the Normans complicated things enormously. England now had to cope with a third language—French, alongside Latin and English—as well as a civil service of French scribes who brought with them a new set of words and spelling conventions. The impact of French on English was huge, and has often been described. Thousands of French words—such as *treasure*, *letter*, and *grace*—entered the language, and many words began to be spelled in different ways. In Anglo-Saxon times there were *cwens* ('kwayns'). Now there were *queens*.

But French did something far more powerful, as far as English usage was concerned. It provided a new linguistic pecking order, with French at the top and English at the bottom. French was the language of the court; English of the common people. A text assigned to the monk Robert of Gloucester makes it clear that, as early as the end of the thirteenth century, there is a clear difference between the language used by upper and lower classes. 'Vor bote a man conne Frenss me telþ of him lute...':

> Unless a man knows French he is thought little of
> And low-born men keep to English, and to their own
> speech still.

No chance of English developing a prestige, standard form in such circumstances. The one thing it *didn't* have was prestige. And in any case, England already had a standard language which guaranteed intelligibility among upper-class people—namely, French.

Trilingual Britain didn't last long. Changing political circumstances—not least, the Hundred Years War between England and France—made French a less palatable option. The effect was soon felt at all levels of society, and knowledge of the language began to diminish. The Cornishman John of Trevisa, writing a hundred years after Robert of Gloucester, has a delightful way of putting it. 'Nowadays', he says, 'children at grammar school know no more French than their left heel.'

English immediately filled the vacuum left by departing French. Latin would continue to be used as the language of the Church and of scholarship, but for most everyday purposes English became the norm. And it adapted, as all languages do, to meet the new circumstances. The presence of a sharply divided class system promoted an upper-class speech, full of ornate French and Latin words and expressions; and this looked and sounded very different from the ordinary language of the lower classes, which was much more Germanic in character. Middle English even provides two ways of describing the contrast: upper-class language was said to be *lered* ('learned'); lower-class was *lewed* ('unlearned'—a word which would later develop an even more negative sense: *lewd*).

People knew what was going on. Several authors write about it. Characters in their stories illustrate it. Careful detective work in Middle English texts brings to light many references to the contrast between what we would today call 'posh' and 'ordinary' talk. There is a nice example in Chaucer, in *The Manciple's Tale*. Phebus' wife has sent for her lover, whom she calls a *lemman*. It evidently wasn't a very elegant word to use at the time, and it immediately makes the narrator utter an apology to the reader:

> Hir lemman? Certes, this is a knayvyssh speche!
> Foryeveth it me, that I yow biseche.

> ['Her lover? Certainly that's a knavish way of talking!
> Forgive it me, I beseech you.']

Some of Chaucer's characters comment in the opposite direction. One in *The Merchant's Tale* doesn't like what he calls *scole-termes* ('school words'). Another, in the epilogue to *The Man of Law's Tale*, says he has *but litel Latyn in my mawe*—'I have little stomach for Latin words'. In *The House of Fame*, a talking eagle—a companion of the god Jupiter—is proud of the fact that he can speak in both styles, learned and unlearned. Although the bird uses many hard words, such as *reparacions* ('reparations') and *dissymulacions* ('dissimulations'), he knows how to talk to ordinary people too. *I can lewedly to a lewed man speke*, he says at one point: 'I know how to talk in an unlearned way to unlearned people.' The eagle can get on with all kinds of people, it seems. He has two dialects at his disposal, and that makes him a much more useful eagle, in acting as a messenger to humanity, than if he had only one.

We can see the origins of today's linguistic conflicts in these early readings. Upper-class people ridicule the way uneducated people speak. Ordinary people ridicule the way educated people speak—though usually at a safe distance. In *The Canterbury Tales* it is for the most part good-humoured banter, with just the occasional explosion. But in the literature of the period we find a harsher language too, and the beginnings of a regional—as distinct from a class—dimension to the conflict.

John of Trevisa was the translator of a well-known Latin work by the Cheshire monk Ranulph Higden called *Polychronicon*—a 'chronicle of many ages'. It was published in 1387, but some of Higden's sources date from the twelfth century. In it, we find an early reference to one part of the country not liking the way they speak in another part:

> All the language of the Northumbrians, and especially at York, is so harsh, piercing, and grating, and formless, that we Southern men may hardly understand it.

And Higden knows why:

> I believe that this is because they are near to outlandish men and foreigners, who speak in a foreign language, and also because the kings of England always live far from that region, being more inclined to the southern part of the country.

And he adds:

> The reason why they are more in the south than the north may
> be better cornland, more people, more noble cities, and more
> profitable harbours.

For his first reason, he may well have been thinking
about the Scots and their use of Gaelic—not a very plausible
explanation, given the great distance between York and
Edinburgh. The descendants of the Danes were doubtless
some of those he called 'outlandish'. But his second reason
is exactly right. Already, by the end of the twelfth century,
the south-east was becoming a region of special political,
social, economic, and cultural influence. It was all happening in London—and later, in Oxford and Cambridge. And
to copy the way courtiers and scholars talked—but especially the former—was being perceived to be the best way
to get on in society.

When one part of a country becomes the centre of
prestige, because it contains the capital city, it is not surprising to find that class and region interact, so that other parts
of the country begin to be called (in a negative sense)
'provincial'. Provincial in geography quickly transmutes into
provincial in dress, manners, and other forms of behaviour,
especially speech. And the further away from the capital,
the more provincial you are deemed to be.

For English in England, distance had to mean 'south' versus
'far north'. (There was no 'far east'—only the North Sea—and
the 'far west' was a totally different story, being populated
by dragons, and the Celtic-speaking Cornish and Welsh.)

The south/north divide, linguistically, was very real. The north had been the area where most of the Vikings had settled, in Anglo-Saxon times. It was a region full of Danish place-names and personal names—*Brandsby, Skewsby, Oadby... Davidson, Jackson, Johnson...* —and the dialects contained many Norse words that hadn't spread south, such as *gleg* ('quick, sharp'), *addle* ('earn'), and *kirk* ('church'). The Vikings may have gone from Britain, but they had left a lot of their local language behind them.

Ranulph Higden doesn't like what the Danes did to English, and he says so very forcibly:

> by intermingling and mixing, first with Danes and afterwards with Normans, in many people the language of the land is harmed, and some use strange inarticulate utterance, chattering, snarling, and harsh teeth-gnashing.

The words sound much better in Middle English—*strange wlaffing, chyteryng, harryng, and garryng grisbittyng*. But this quotation is of especial interest, because it says something more than just 'they speak funny up north'. Higden doesn't like Danes; but he doesn't like Normans either. It isn't just Danish words he objects to, but French words too. And French words were being widely used in London, as well as up north.

This is the beginning of another strand in the tradition of linguistic complaint: an antagonism to foreign words as such. Higden thinks the character of English has been harmed by the thousands of loan words that had been coming into the language since the Norman Conquest. We would have to agree that the foreign words certainly changed the character of English. But harmed it? On the contrary, it allowed the language to develop fresh dimensions of expression. As we will see in a later chapter, without all those French (and Latin) words, there would have been no Chaucer, and no Shakespeare, as we know them.

And no Higden either. Without French words, he would not even have been able to write the above sentences. For example, he says: 'the language of the land is harmed'. In the original text this appears as *þe contray longage ys apeyred*. All three main words here—*country, language, appair* (modern *impair*)—are loan words from French.

All languages borrow from each other. It is one of the linguistic facts of life. We know of no 'pure' language—that is, one which has a homogeneous linguistic character, displaying no influence from the contact its speakers have had with other languages. To adopt an analogy from the American political domain, the linguistic world has many of the characteristics of a melting-pot, rather than a salad-bowl. But there is a long-standing salad-bowl attitude, which is found in several countries, that it is a good thing to keep languages free from foreign influences. It is an attitude which can be traced back to classical languages such as Latin. In English it surfaces for the first time in the fourteenth century. And it becomes a major issue 200 years later.

Upper-class vs. lower-class. North vs. south. Native vs. foreign. The linguistic scene was getting complicated. And it was about to get even more so. Seventy-six years after the death of Chaucer, in 1400, William Caxton introduced his printing-press.

3

Variations

THE arrival of printing changed the goal-posts. It introduced a new set of criteria to be taken into account when deciding questions of usage. And it presented William Caxton with a linguistic problem.

He tells us all about it in the prologue to *The Booke of Eneydos*—a translation of Virgil's *Aeneid*. It seems that a shipload of sailors were becalmed in the Thames estuary, and while they waited for the wind to change they went ashore to get something to eat. This is how Caxton tells it. (I have modernized his spelling and punctuation, apart from the way he spells the two critical words for 'eggs'.)

> and one of them, named Sheffield, a mercer, came into a house and asked for meat [food], and especially he asked after *eggys*. And the good wife answered that she could speak no French. And the merchant was angry, for he also could speak no French, but would have had *egges*, and she understood him not. And then at last another said that he would have *eyren*. Then the good wife said that she understood him well.

This kind of communicative breakdown still happens. A modern-day American Sheffield, walking into a British store and asking for *diapers* might be treated with just as much incomprehension as a British Sheffield walking into a US store and asking for *nappies*. But present-day communications, and especially British exposure to American English, have made the problem a small one. Not so for Caxton. He goes on to say:

> Lo, what should a man in these days now write, *egges* or *eyren*? Certainly it is hard to please every man by cause of diversity or change of language.

And in another place, he reflects: 'That common English that is spoken in one shire varyeth from another.'

We know why there were two words for eggs. *Egges* was a northern form, a development from Old Norse. *Eyren* was a southern form, a development from Old English. As a printer, Caxton would have to choose. Today, there isn't so much of a problem. Publishers do what others have done before them, and follow a set of guidelines sanctioned by decades—sometimes centuries—of practice. But Caxton had no one to copy. He was the first.

He knew he might be criticized. Indeed, he already had been. Hard to please every man? Or woman. In the prologue to another book—the first book to be printed in England, *The Recuyell* [compilation] *of the Historyes of Troy*— he reflects on his experience in the translating business. It hadn't been easy. He had, he says, written some forty or fifty pages, then got fed up:

> I fell in despair of this work and purposed no more to have continued therein, and those quires [of paper] laid apart, and in two years after laboured no more in this work.

But then he met Lady Margaret, the sister of King Edward IV, and happened to mention what he had done. She asks to see it, and she likes what she sees:

> she… commanded me straightly to continue and make an end of the residue then not translated.

However, there was a down side:

> And when she had seen them, anon she found a default in my English which she commanded me to amend.

And, knowing on which side his linguistic bread was to be buttered, he corrected it. Lady Margaret: the first English copy-editor.

Deep down, Caxton is proud of his own English. In his prologue he tells his readers so:

> I… was born and learned my English in Kent in the Weald, where I doubt not is spoken as broad and rude English as in any place in England.

Rude meant no more than 'unpolished'. It was a conventional expression used by writers who were being humble about their usage. A nod to the reader, really: your English is *much* better than mine… Caxton was being a wise businessman. He wanted his book to sell.

And sell it did. He printed the 700-page *Recuyell* in Bruges, in 1473–4, then set up a printing-house in London, somewhere in the precincts of Westminster Abbey, to be near the court. He must have been doing well: he paid a year's rent in advance for his premises. And by the time of his death, in about 1491, he had published over a hundred books, including two editions of *The Canterbury Tales*—best-sellers, by the standards of the time.

The impact on people's developing sense of English usage must have been powerful. For the first time, a single text was in front of the eyes of thousands of people, and in a medium which was much easier to read than had hitherto been the case. The handwritten manuscripts which had been the earlier practice were, by their nature, fewer in number, limited in distribution, and very variable in linguistic character. Ælfric had worried about the inefficiency of copyists. So had Chaucer, who actually went so far—though doubtless with tongue in cheek—as to wish disease on his copyist, Adam, if he did not improve his skills.

> Adam scriveyn, if ever it thee befalle
> Boece or Troylus for to wryten newe,
> Under thy long lokkes thou mow have the scalle,
> But after my makyng thou wryte more trewe;
> So ofte a-daye I mot thy werk renewe,
> It to correcte and eek to rubbe and scrape,
> And al is thorough thy negligence and rape.

['Adam copyist, if ever it comes about that you have to write out again Boece or Troilus, under your long locks of hair you shall get the scabs, unless you write more accurately according to my composition. So often every day I have to revise your work, to correct it and also to rub out and scrape out; and all because of your negligence and haste.']

Generations of Chaucer editors have regretted the fact that the advice was not taken up as thoroughly as the author would have liked. The extant manuscripts are full of copyist variations, so much so that it is sometimes impossible to decide what Chaucer's original text must have been. Nor did the printers entirely solve the problem: there were negligent typesetters too. But there is no doubt that printing added an element of linguistic stability to literature. Slowly, the climate for the emergence of a standard language was being formed. But the 'diversity' that Caxton was aware of was a huge barrier to progress.

The Middle Ages had seen a wondrous flowering of regional dialects in England. Local communities evolved as the population grew, and new accents and dialects were the natural consequence. At a time when even small geographical distances were barriers to communication, it is not surprising to find texts being written, even within a few dozen miles of each other, which reflect local sounds, words, and grammar.

Here's an example of the extent of the problem. Take an everyday word like *might*, as in *I might go*. Over twenty different spellings have been recorded for this word in Middle English—a baker's dozen is *meahte, mœhte, mihte, micte, myhte, michte, miitte, myht, mahte, mihhte, miȝte, mighte,* and *myght*. Thousands of words had variants. How had such extensive variation arisen?

Imagine you are a scribe living in Lincoln in the early 1400s. Your daily work consists of composing or copying documents of all kinds for administrative, legal, religious, literary, and other clients. You have to spell words as best you can. You are on your own, apart perhaps from some fellow scribes—who are in the same position as you are. If a word comes up that you do not know, there are no dictionaries to turn to, to decide on a spelling. You have to write the word down as you think it ought to be spelled. You may sound it out first. The likelihood is that the spelling will reflect features of your local Lincolnshire accent.

Alternatively, you may have built up your own code of 'good practice' from the documents you have read in the past. Certain words will recur in your work, and you will have developed a favourite way of spelling them. You might even keep a list. If you are stuck, you can always ask other Lincoln scribes, over a late-night pot of ale, and do what they do. You might even remember a word turning up in Chaucer, or the Bible, and write it in the same way.

Even if you are copying, you will unconsciously add variations. You will, without realizing it, 'translate' the spellings in a document into the conventions you know best. This still happens today. If I ask an American to copy the sentence *The plate was decorated with all the colours of the rainbow*, they will almost always write *colors* for *colours*, without noticing. And British copyists, presented with *colors*, will do the reverse. It all depends on what you are used to. And in Middle England, what most people were used to was very much a local world. If a document written in a Kentish scriptorium arrived in Lincoln to be copied, its Kentishisms would very likely be altered. A scribe might even deliberately turn things into a style that would be more intelligible to the good burghers of Lincoln.

Now imagine this happening over a century or more, all over the country. The number of local variations is going to be vast. It's wonderful evidence for modern dialectologists trying to find out about Middle English dialects, of course. But for the people of the time, there was a steadily growing problem of mutual intelligibility. All writers must have been worried, but civil servants, lawyers, and literary authors most of all.

The problem was for the reader, not for the writer. As an author I can write the word *poor* as *poor*, *poore*, *pore*, *powr*, *power*, *puer*, *pur*, *puur*, *pure*, and in many other ways. Because I am the writer, I know what I mean. But you, as the reader, you have to work it out for yourself. If you read *The kinge has a puer companion*, what is it supposed to mean? Is it *poor* or *pure*—or even *power(ful)*? If there are too many words which overlap in spelling, or which are identical ('homographs'), your ability to read efficiently will collapse. Context will often help you work out what is going on, but not always. And the whole task becomes much more difficult than it should be.

Very few writers have left comments reflecting their worries about the way language diversity might affect their work. But Chaucer was one. At the end of *Troilus and Criseyde*, in an address to his 'litel bok', he writes:

> And for there is so gret diversite
> In Englissh and in writyng of our tonge
> So prey I God that non myswrite the

['And because there is so great diversity in English and in the writing of our tongue, so pray I God that none miswrite you']

He was right to be worried. The scale of the problem was increasing. At the end of the Old English period, there were about 50,000 words in the language. By the end of the Middle English period, in the fifteenth century, this total had doubled. There were lots of unfamiliar foreign words, too, as we have seen. People could not carry on spelling these words any way they wanted. In a country that was becoming increasingly centralized, with London as a national capital, there had to be a standard. People had to agree, at least, about how words were to be spelled.

Things could not go on like this. William Caxton had to make one set of decisions, when he began to publish. But a standard language cannot evolve overnight. In fact, it would take three hundred years.

4

Standards

A linguistically or dialectally diverse nation needs a standard language to permit mutual intelligibility. Nor is it just a nation. In a global society, it is the whole world that can benefit from a lingua franca. Latin once took on this role, at least among Western nations. French too has played its part as an international medium of communication. Today, English is the dominant global voice.

Whatever 'standard English' is, it is of relevance not just for Britain, but for all countries that want to talk to each other. If the United Nations is seen as an index of communicative intent, that means (in 2006) 191 nations. There are serious implications for usage here, as we shall see in due course. But in 1400, we are talking about just one nation, England—or Britain, if we allow that English had established itself in Scotland, Ireland, and Wales as a result of the political initiatives of the previous 200 years. How did the standard language develop here? And why?

There is nothing inherently complicated about the notion of a standard. We use it every day in relation to weights and measures. A standard exists to avoid the dangers of variability.

If coins varied in their weight and size from one part of the country to another, forgers would have a field day. But what does the notion mean when applied to language?

In language, variation causes problems of comprehension and acceptability. If you speak or write differently from the way I do, we may fail to understand each other, and we may also decide not to like each other. The differences may be slight or great. In Middle England, as we have seen in Chapter 3, the gap was becoming increasingly wide. And it was chiefly being noticed in relation to the written language.

There is a very close association between a standard language and writing—in the broadest sense of *writing*, to include handwriting, typewriting, printing, and electronic media. This is because the written language is something which can be controlled. It is not a natural medium of language, as speech is. It has to be learned, through formal processes of teaching, usually in school. If a country is to have a standard language, it has to be taught. And writing is the best medium for introducing it.

It is in any case the written medium that most needs to be standardized. Ambiguities in speech can be quickly cleared up. If you are talking to me, and you use a word I don't know, or you express yourself unclearly, I have the immediate option of asking you what you meant. I can even show you my lack of comprehension while you are talking, by using facial expressions and query vocalizations (*m?, huh?*). Communication theorists call this behaviour 'simultaneous feedback'. Conversation would break down without it.

But there is no simultaneous feedback in writing. How you are reacting to the paragraph you are reading now, I, as its author, will never know—unless one day you write and tell me, and that doesn't help me while I am writing it. Right now, I have no idea how it is going to be received. So I must make every effort to make it clear, able to stand on its own feet. Writing has an autonomy that conversation does not need, which is where a standard language comes in. It helps ensure that my communicative intentions will meet your requirements and expectations. Now that we have a standard, to dipaart frm it wood intradjoos unecesri difkulti.

The equivalent of that last clause was perfectly possible in Middle English. And in it we can see the primary feature of a standard variety of a language. It is the spelling. There are other important elements in a standard, as we shall see—notably punctuation and grammar—but spelling is the critical thing. Nowadays, we can get away with a certain flexibility in punctuation, and also in grammar, but there is very little leeway in spelling. With just one or two exceptions (such as informal emails), if you spell incorrectly you will, nowadays, be considered careless, lazy, or uneducated, or possibly all three.

But that is a modern notion. It didn't exist in the Middle Ages. It took three hundred years for standard English to develop into something like the form we know today, and for modern criticisms of non-standard usage to be formulated. We shall see the standard language coming into its own in the eighteenth century. And after that, as they say in the movies, all hell breaks loose.

It is in the fifteenth century that we see the first signs of the emerging standard. Thanks to years of persistent research in historical linguistics, it is possible to detect a definite trend towards consistency in the documents from many London institutions of the time, especially among the scribes of the court of Chancery. It was fostered by the wide dissemination of a few important texts, especially after the arrival of printing—chief among them were Chaucer's *Canterbury Tales* and John Wycliffe's translation of the Bible. The linguistic features of one dialect—that of the east midlands, and notably of the London area—began to predominate. And in due course it is this dialect which forms the basis of the standard language.

The momentum towards a standard gathers pace during the fifteenth century. But this raises a question. Why did it take so long for it to happen? It wasn't just the late arrival of printing. There have to be more fundamental reasons.

It couldn't really have happened much earlier. A standard presupposes a certain level of stability in a language. And in Middle English, that stability wasn't there. It was a period when the language was rapidly changing—not only in vocabulary, with tens of thousands of new words arriving from French, Latin, and elsewhere, but also in grammar, spelling, and pronunciation. Each of these areas was in a considerable state of flux.

Since Anglo-Saxon times, a major shift had taken place in the way English grammar worked. In Old English, the language had used many word-endings (inflections) to express the grammatical relationships between words.

In Middle English, these had largely disappeared, and English was beginning to rely on the order of words in a sentence to express meaning. But it takes time for a language to settle down, after such a major shift in its patterns of sentence construction. We can see the reverberations of the upheaval even as late as 1600, when Shakespeare was writing. He was, for instance, one of the last writers to make extensive use, outside of religion, of the old contrast between the pronouns *thou* and *you* and the associated inflection (*thou knowest*).

In spelling, the language was assimilating the consequences of having a civil service of French scribes, who paid little attention to the traditions of English spelling that had developed in Anglo-Saxon times. Not only did French *qu* arrive, replacing Old English *cw* (as in *queen*), but *ch* replaced *c* (in such words as *church*—Old English *cirice*), *sh* and *sch* replaced *sc* (as in *ship*—Old English *scip*), and much more. Vowels were written in a great number of ways. Much of the irregularity of modern English spelling derives from the forcing together of Old English and French systems of spelling in the Middle Ages. People struggled to find the best way of writing English throughout the period—and without much success, as we shall see in the next chapter. Even Caxton didn't help, at times. Some of his typesetters were Dutch, and they introduced some of their own spelling conventions into their work. That is where the *gh* in such words as *ghost* comes from.

Any desire to standardize spelling would also have been hindered by the major changes that were taking place in pronunciation during the Middle English period, especially in the fifteenth century. A series of changes affecting the long vowels of English, known as the Great Vowel Shift, took place in the early 1400s. Before the shift, a word like *loud* would have been pronounced 'lood'; *name* as 'nahm'; *leaf* as 'layf'; *mice* as 'mees'. Although the shift had no clear beginning or end, the majority of the changes took place within two generations. Grandparents and grandchildren in 1450 probably had considerable difficulty understanding each other.

We can easily see the problem that a period of rapid pronunciation change presents for the emergence of a standard system of spelling. If some people are pronouncing *name* as 'nahm' and some are beginning to say something closer to 'naym', then how is it to be spelled? Only after the pace of change had slowed, towards the end of the century, would the introduction of standard spellings have begun to make any sense.

But once the linguistic climate of a country is ready for a standard, and once a particular dialect has emerged as a favoured candidate, the process is impossible to stop. This does not mean that its progress is steady, unidirectional, and uncontroversial. On the contrary. Caxton couldn't have predicted it, but within a few decades of his death, the country was having to cope with some of the biggest rows in the history of English usage.

5

Reformers

I F there are no rules, it is difficult to complain about them being broken. And linguistic rules can only be formulated when people have a clear intuition about normal usage. If usage is highly varied and rapidly changing, as it was in much of Middle English, then it is extremely difficult to work out what the rules are. That was Caxton's problem. There were no spelling manuals, guides to punctuation, grammars, or dictionaries of English in the fifteenth century. But a generation later, things had settled down considerably. People started to reflect on what had been happening. And then they began to complain about it.

Spelling, inevitably, was the first target. There was a growing opinion among the intelligentsia that English spelling was a mess. The Chester Herald, John Hart, was one of the strongest critics. He wrote three books advocating spelling reform, one of which shows his opinion in its title: *The Opening of the Unreasonable Writing of our Inglish Toung*, published in 1551. The spelling system was unreasonable, he argues—based on no rational principle. The language is full of 'vices and corruptions'. It had to be sorted out: 'confusion and disorder' in spelling 'bringeth confusion and uncertainte in the reading'.

What sort of thing was Hart referring to? It wasn't just the arrival of French spellings. It was also the way in which well-intentioned people had tried to help, and added to the confusion. The renewed interest in classical languages and cultures, which formed part of the ethos of the Renaissance, had introduced a new perspective into spelling: etymology. Etymology is the study of the history of words, and there was a widespread view that words should show their history in the way they were spelled. These weren't classicists showing off. There was a genuine belief that it would help people if they could 'see' the original Latin in a Latin-derived English word.

So someone added a *b* to the word typically spelled *det*, *dett*, or *dette* in Middle English, because the source in Latin was *debitum*, and it became *debt*, and caught on. Similarly, an *o* was added to *peple*, because it came from *populum*: we find both *poeple* and *people*, before the latter became the norm. An *s* was added to *ile* and *iland*, because of Latin *insula*, so we now have *island*. There are many more such cases. Some people nowadays find it hard to understand why there are so many 'silent letters' of this kind in English. It is because other people thought they were helping.

Hart didn't like this kind of scholarly interference. Nor did he much like what the printers had been up to. Although Caxton had made a series of decisions about spelling, not everyone followed them. Indeed, Caxton had been very inconsistent himself. In his texts we find *wyf* alongside *wyfe* ('wife'), *lytyl* alongside *lityl* ('little'), *good* alongside *goode*, and many more alternatives. Even his own typesetters went their own way, at times. They made arbitrary decisions. If a line of type was a bit short on a page, well, just add an -*e* to a few words, and that will fill it out. And if a line was too long? Take out some *e*'s, and then it will fit.

There is a good case for saying that, far from the arrival of printing helping the standard language to emerge, it actually hindered it, because there was so much inconsistency. Even a century after Caxton, the printers were still in a muddle. The headteacher of Merchant Taylors' school, Richard Mulcaster—said to be the model for Holofernes in *Love's Labour's Lost*—was so unimpressed by printing practice that he decided to base his spelling rules on handwritten texts and not printed ones, because 'the printers, setters, and correcters … letteth manie errors abide in their work'.

We can hardly blame foreign typesetters for getting into a muddle and manipulating the language in this way. They would have had no intuition about what would count as an error. The case of final -*e* must have really confused them. They were printing at a time when -*e* was sometimes found at the end of a word and sometimes not. Sometimes it was pronounced and sometimes it wasn't. For example, we are still not entirely sure how many *e*'s were sounded in the first line of *The Canterbury Tales*—'When April with its sweet showers'…

Whan that Aprille with hise shoures soote…

The metre suggests that there is no -*e* pronounced in *Aprille* and *hise*, but that there is one in *shoures*—'shoor-uhs'. But people disagree over whether *soote* was 'soht' or 'soht-uh'.

A foreign compositor would get the impression that final -*e* was random, and that he could put it in or leave it out as he wished.

The situation would not be helped at all by the arrival of the Renaissance and the growth in international exploration and trade. New waves of foreign words came into the language, during the sixteenth and seventeenth centuries, and they brought with them unfamiliar pronunciations and alien letter-combinations. Thousands of words arrived from Latin and Greek, and many of them looked very strange in an English alphabet, such as *encyclopaedia* and *vacuum*. There were more words from French, such as *bizarre* and *moustache*. Words came in from Italian and Spanish— *piazza*, *macaroni*, *cocoa*, *guitar*. And hundreds of loan words arrived, from over a dozen languages, whose alien spellings added further complication to the already complex English system: *yacht* (Dutch), *yoghurt* (Turkish), *bazaar* (Persian), *pariah* (Tamil), *sheikh* (Arabic)... In all of this, we are not talking small numbers. A vocabulary of around 100,000 words at the end of Middle English had more than doubled by 1700. As a consequence, the number of 'exceptions to the rules' hugely increased.

But even in the early decades of the sixteenth century, readers were being faced with many spelling variations, and Hart identifies several major problems which he would like to eliminate. He especially objects to unnecessary letters, as when *good* is spelled *goode*, or cases where a sound is spelled by more than one letter, such as *set* spelled as *sette*. And he hates silent letters, as in *debt* and *people*. He is an early phonetician, arguing vehemently for 'one sound—one letter'—so he is against having the same letter *g*, for example, in both *gentle* and *together*. The spelling system he devised proposed several new symbols and conventions to sort out the muddle. They never caught on. After Hart's time, only two new symbol innovations were ever accepted: *i* eventually came to be distinguished from *j*, and *u* from *v*. The English alphabet grew from twenty-four letters to twenty-six. And it has stayed that way.

Why weren't Hart's ideas for radical reform successful? The problem was that he was not alone. There were several other spelling reformers with the bit between their teeth, and each of them ended up with a proposal of their own. No two systems agreed as to what would be the best way of 'improving' English spelling. And there is in any case a natural reluctance to adopt an inventor's new and unfamiliar symbols. It was to be the same in the twentieth century, when George Bernard Shaw and others raised the case for spelling reform again. Spelling reformers have always been divided amongst themselves.

Nonetheless, the widespread opposition in the sixteenth century to 'too many letters' did influence publishing practice. The extra consonant and final *e* in words like *goode*, *sette*, and *hadde* eventually died out. It did not take long. Hart died in 1574. Within fifty years such spellings had almost disappeared. In the First Folio of Shakespeare (1623) we find 1,398 instances of *had* and only one of *hadde*.

If radical reform was not the way to sort out spelling, what was the alternative? Richard Mulcaster presented it, in a work called *The Elementarie* (1582), a treatise on the principles of early education. He took the view that things had gone too far to be radically changed. Although English began with 'one letter—one sound', he argues, too much has happened since Anglo-Saxon times, so that introducing a phonetic approach would be unworkable. Better, he says, to deal with what we have—the established letters—and gather the words together, making adjustments where needed. Custom, he insists, is 'a great and naturall governour'. So, he concludes, let us gather all the 'roaming rules' that custom has introduced into English, and organize them into a single work.

He wasn't just a theoretician. He started the job off himself, creating an alphabetical list of over 8,500 words with recommended spellings, based on what he saw people using in their handwritten texts. It was almost a dictionary, but not quite, for it wasn't a systematic guide to meanings. His judgements were remarkably prescient. If we compare the words in his list with the standard spellings we use today, we find that over half are the same. And most of the differences are either due to the emergence of *i/j* and *u/v* or are minor variants at the ends of words, as in *elementarie* and *equall*.

The arguments about spelling reform died away, by the end of the sixteenth century, and the spelling system began to settle down. But it still had a long way to go before it reached the present-day level of standardization, and there would be several vacillating fashions in the meantime. In the late seventeenth century, for instance, it became fashionable—following a trend in printing in Continental Europe—to capitalize the first letter of nouns. Virtually every noun is capitalized in Jonathan Swift's *Baucis and Philemon*, for example, written in 1706:

> In antient Time, as Story tells
> The Saints would often leave their Cells,
> And strole about, but hide their Quality,
> To try the People's Hospitality.

The practice lasted for a century or so, then died out—or rather, it was killed off, as we shall see (Chapter 24).

Even in Dr Johnson's *Dictionary*, published as recently as 1755, there are many words spelled differently from today's norms—for instance, *fewel* ('fuel'), *villany*, *raindeer*, *downfal*, *comick*... And that work still groups together words spelled with *i/j* and *u/v*, so that, in Johnson's alphabetical listing, *ejectment* comes before *eight* and *avast* precedes *auction*.

It took nearly four hundred years, between 1400 and 1800, for English spelling to reach the kind of steady state that Mulcaster wanted to see. But even in 1800—or, for that matter, in 2000—there was more spelling variation remaining than we might realize. I'll be looking at this later (Chapter 21)—and also reflecting on the irony that, just as people thought they had sorted the spelling system out, something happened which began to mess it up again.

6

Borrowings

Rows over spelling continued throughout the 1500s. But they were a mild breeze compared with the tempestuous quarrels which took place that century over other aspects of language. Not over grammar and punctuation—those rows came later—but over vocabulary.

It is always dangerous generalizing about an age, but there is no doubt that during the sixteenth century anxiety levels about language increased greatly. There developed an intensity of interest in linguistic matters which had not been seen before. What caused it? The movement towards a standard language was not the reason. English was beginning to evolve a standard form, as we have seen, but there was no row about it. That came later. Indeed, the term 'standard language' is not recorded in English until the early nineteenth century.

The anxieties were more deep-rooted. They arose as a result of the huge cultural changes which had been taking place since the Middle Ages. The period from the time of Caxton until around 1650 would later be called the Renaissance—the rebirth of learning. It was a period which included the Reformation (Luther's protest at Wittenberg was 1517), Copernicus (his major work was published in 1543), the first encounters with Africa and the Americas, and a renewal of connection with classical languages and literatures. Language never exists in a vacuum: it is always a reflection of cultural change. And if there is serious discord about that change, there will be serious discord about the language used to express it.

The discord that we now call the Reformation had immediate consequences for English, in the form of new translations of the Bible into the vernacular. John Wycliffe's translation had been the first, as early as the 1380s. But the first English text to be printed was the New Testament of William Tyndale, published in 1525-6. By 1611, when the King James Bible appeared, over fifty different Protestant or Catholic English translations had been made.

There were heated arguments over the linguistic choices made by the translators. Charges of heresy could be levelled at a translation depending on whether it used *congregation* or *church*, *repentance* or *penance*, *charity* or *love*. Sir Thomas More condemned Tyndale for 'certain wordes euille [evil] & of euyll purpose changid'. What words? More didn't like the way Tyndale used *senior* instead of *priest*—to take just one example. We can see theological concerns here. But he also didn't like Tyndale's choice of some quite everyday words too. For instance, he castigates him for mixing up 'two so plain englishe wordes, and so commen [common] as is *naye* and *no*'.

Tyndale thought things were going too far, and said so. His critics, he says, 'haue yet now so narowlye loked [looked] on my translatyon, that there is not so much as one I therin if it lack a tytle [tittle] over his hed, but they haue noted it, and nombre it vnto the ignorant people for an heresy'. He can't even leave a dot off the letter *i* without someone calling him a heretic, it seems.

One of the issues which exercised the minds of the early Bible translators was: would the English language be able to cope? For a start, were there enough words available to express everything that was said in the Latin or Greek originals? In the early decades of the sixteenth century, the general opinion was that there weren't. The traveller and physician Andrew Boorde wrote in about 1550: 'The speche of Englande is a base speche [compared] to other noble speches, as Italion Castylion [Spanish] and Frenche... ' And there is a famous poem by John Skelton in which he bemoans his fate if he should choose to write in an ornate style, as appears in French and Latin poets:

> Our Language is so rustye,
> So cankered and so ful
> Of frowardes [ugly things] and so dul
> That if I wold [would] apply
> To write ornatly
> I wot [know] not where to finde
> Termes to serve my minde.

If the problem was obvious, so was the solution. If the classical languages had all the words needed to talk about everything, and English hadn't, then all writers had to do was borrow. 'Borrow' is not the most apposite of terms for what happens, in such cases, for the receiving language does not give the words back. 'Share' is perhaps more appropriate. But the tradition is to talk of 'loan words' and not 'shared words', in such cases. Certainly, whatever we call them, the sixteenth century saw an extraordinary influx of new words from Latin and Greek, especially the former: *anonymous, appropriate, commemorate, emancipate, relevant, susceptible*...

Many writers, such as the diplomat Thomas Elyot, embraced the new loan words with enthusiasm. We have to have them, he insists in 1531, 'for the necessary augmentation of our langage'. A generation later, in 1581, the translator George Pettie reaffirms their importance. We couldn't talk at all without them, he says:

> if they should be all counted inkpot termes, I know not how we should speake any thing without blacking our mouthes with inke.

Inkpot terms. *Inkhorn* terms. These two words, both meaning a receptacle for ink, arrived in English at that time. Pettie is using a locution which had become common in the middle decades of the century. *Inkpot term* is first recorded in 1553, *inkhorn term* in 1543. Applied to language, they refer to words which are so lengthy (because of their foreign origins) that to write them down would use up a lot of ink. Accordingly, 'inkhorn terms' became an abusive label to describe the writing of anyone who welcomed Latinate neologisms, and especially for those who overused them.

There are certainly many examples of the style of writing which was thought to be excessively Latinate. In 1553, the scholar Thomas Wilson cites a letter—he may have concocted it, but it illustrates his point—supposedly written by a Lincolnshire gentleman. It contains such passages as:

> how could you haue adepted suche illustrate prerogatiue and dominicall superioritee if the fecunditee of your ingenie had not been so fertile, and wounderfull pregnaunt.

> ['how could you have acquired such illustrious pre-eminence and lordly superiority, if the fecundity of your intellectual powers had not been so fertile and wonderfully pregnant?']

Faced with such usage, it is not surprising to see the pendulum swing to the opposite extreme, in which such coinages are avoided like the plague. Even a scholar of Greek, Sir John Cheke, was hotly opposed to them. In a 1557 letter he writes:

> I am of this opinion that our tung shold [should] be written cleane and pure, vnmixt and vnmangeled with borowing of other tunges.

It is a view strongly espoused by Wilson. We should never, he says, 'affect any straunge ynkehorne termes, but to speake as is commonly received'. And he adds, wryly:

> Some seeke so far for outlandish English, that they forget altogether their mothers language. And I dare sweare this, if some of their mothers were aliue, thei were not able to tell what they say.

The row went on for half a century—and indeed it has been rumbling on ever since. Four hundred years later,

George Orwell would be haranguing people for their reliance on classical words:

> Bad writers… are nearly always haunted by the notion that Latin or Greek words are grander than Saxon ones.

And in the nineteenth century, the Dorset poet William Barnes went so far as to propose the removal of *all* non-Germanic words from the language. In his own writing, he replaced *conscience* by *inwit*, *ornithology* by *birdlore*, *grammar* by *speechcraft*, and many more.

Both sides of the inkhorn controversy had a point, and the extremists on both sides obscured it. Quite plainly, the routine use of classical terms makes for a style of English which is far removed from everyday speech, and which would be tolerable (and even then, not always) only in specialist circumstances such as the law. On the other hand, there are many classical terms which have been thoroughly assimilated into everyday speech, so much so that it would be very hard to talk for long without using them. That one sentence quoted above from John Cheke, arguing against foreign words, actually uses four of them: *opinion*, *pure*, *mix*, and *mangle*—all from Latin via Old French. And it is the same with Orwell: *haunt*, *notion*, *grand*.

Extreme trends in language use tend to be ironed out over time. Languages seem to operate with an unconsciously held system of checks and balances. If a group of people go wildly off in one linguistic direction, using a crate of new words, eventually—if they want to continue as part of society and be understood by its other members—they

will be pulled back, and they will drop some of their neologisms. At the same time, a few of the new words will have
been picked up by the rest of the community. And so a
language grows.

This is what happened in the sixteenth century. As a
result of the inkhorn controversy, many of the classical
neologisms fell out of use. It is thought that as many as a
third of all the new words which came into English at that
time are not recorded after 1700. We no longer use *accersite*
'summon', *dominical* 'lordly', and *suppeditate* 'supply', to
cite just three. On the other hand, the foreign words that
did remain added greatly to the expressive richness of
English, and were put to very good use by writers who
exploited their stylistic nuances and rhythmical differences.
A language which can *question* (from French) and *interrogate*
(from Latin) as well as *ask* (Old English) is three times more
expressive in that respect than a language which can only
'ask'. And the same applies to *rest*, *remainder*, and *residue*, and
many more such 'triplets'. Listen to them in Shakespeare,
and judge for yourself:

    ... the residue of your fortune (*As You Like It*, II. vii. 200)
    ... upon remainder of a dear account (*Richard II*, I. i. 130)
    ... the rest is silence (*Hamlet*, v. ii. 352)

7

Courtiers

B Y the end of the sixteenth century, the inkhorn battle was over. It was widely felt that the language had made up for its deficiencies. And the fact that it contained a mixture of words from other languages began to be seen as a strength rather than a weakness.

We see the point made repeatedly. The courtier Philip Sidney was quite forthright, in his *Defence of Poesie* (1595):

> I knowe some will say it is a mingled language: And why not, so much the better, taking the best of both the other?

Ten years later, William Camden—a friend of Sidney and tutor of Ben Jonson—makes the point that English is now no different from any other language:

> Whereas our tongue is mixed, it is no disgrace, whenas all the tongues of *Europe* doe participate interchangeably the one or the other; and in the learnèd tongues, there hath been like borrowing one from another.

And another decade later, we find poet and antiquary Richard Carew stating what many people were beginning to feel:

> the longe wordes that wee borrowe, being intermingled with the shorte of our owne store, make vp a perfitt harmonye.

A perfect harmony. A strong claim. But there was no shortage of people ready to write books to demonstrate the point. Handbooks of rhetoric were published, modelled on those that had been used for Latin, to show how English could be just as sophisticated in its usage. A principle of 'decorum' was widely advocated. English should display proportion, harmony, brevity, order, naturalness, and vitality. No matter that it was virtually impossible to define such terms clearly. They would be demonstrated by good practice. If everyone felt that a piece of writing was 'harmonious', then it was—even if they were unable to say in what exactly the harmony existed.

And there was good practice a-plenty by the year 1600. The literary hiatus since the time of Chaucer had been ended by the poetry of Edmund Spenser, the plays of Marlowe and Shakespeare, and the drama, poetry, and prose of many other writers. 'Elizabethan literature', as we now call it, demonstrated the expressiveness of English in unprecedented ways. When people look back at the history of the English language and talk nostalgically of a 'golden age', it is usually the age of Shakespeare that they cite. And one of the catch-phrases beloved by modern usage pundits concerned about present-day trends is the one echoing Wordsworth: we must 'preserve the tongue that Shakespeare spoke'.

Was it a golden age? It was, if you happened to be in the right place and belonged to the right class. George Puttenham, who published *The Arte of Poesie* in 1589, tells us exactly what place this was. He is advising poets on the kind of language they should use if they want to be successful. And he is in no doubt. A poet's language should be 'natural, pure, and the most usual of all his country'. So where is this to be found?

> in the kings Court, or in the good townes and Cities within the land, then [rather than] in the marches and frontiers, or in port townes, where straungers haunt for traffike sake, or yet in Vniuersities where Scholers vse much peeuish affectation of words out of the primitiue languages, or finally, in any vplandish village or corner of a Realme, where is no resort but of poore rusticall or vnciuill people.

The ideal norm is evidently aristocratic usage. University types are excluded, thanks to their peevish affectations. And even within the 'good towns and cities', the poet needs to be careful to find the right class of person:

> neither shall he follow the speach of a craftes man or carter, or other of the inferiour sort, though he be inhabitant or bred in the best town and Citie in this Realme, for such persons do abuse good speaches by strange accents or illshapen soundes, and false ortographie. But he shall follow generally the better brought vp sort, such as the Greekes call *charientes*, men ciuill and graciously behauoured and bred.

Strange accents. Ill-shaped sounds. Plainly, poets should not be using regionalisms—even if well-bred people use them:

> neither shall he take the termes of Northern-men, such as they vse in dayly talke, whether they be noble men or gentlemen, or of their best clerkes... nor in effect any speach vsed beyond the riuer of Trent, though no man can deny but that theirs is

the purer English Saxon at this day, yet it is not so Courtly nor so currant as our Southerne English is, no more is the far Westerne mans speach.

North of the River Trent? North of Watford, we would say today. And Puttenham sums it all up with a geographical estimate:

ye shall therfore take the vsuall speach of the Court, and that of London and the shires lying about London within lx. myles, and not much aboue.

Sixty miles. Actually, that was quite generous, for a 60-mile circle around London would include not only Oxford and Cambridge, but also Ipswich and the whole of Kent, where regional dialects were very much in evidence. But Puttenham is not talking about everyone who lives in those areas—only 'the gentlemen and also their learnèd clarkes' who 'speake but specially write as good Southerne as we of Middlesex or Surrey do'. That narrows it down again.

The linguistic prestige of the south-east of England was undisputed. Writing just a couple of years before Puttenham, the topographer William Harrison acknowledges the excellent balance between foreign and native words (Chapter 6) that English had managed to achieve:

ours is a meane [in between] language, and neither too rough nor too smooth in vtterance.

But where is this excellence to be found? In one place only:

the south part of this Iland.

Puttenham's is one of the earliest and fullest accounts we have of what 'good English' was supposed to be. For him, as for Harrison, it was to be found only in the court, in upper-class London, and in the nearby counties. And that, we might think, is that. But no.

Puttenham has a few other things to say about good usage, and things turn out to be a bit more complicated. It transpires that no one should be complacent—not even those to whom one would expect to turn for guidance: the writers and the schoolteachers. They all make mistakes. Puttenham hopes he is not being impertinent, but

> we finde in our English writers many wordes and speaches amendable, & ye shall see in some many inkhorne termes so ill affected brought in by men of learning as preachers and schoolemasters: and many straunge termes of other languages by Secretaries and Marchaunts and trauailours [travellers], and many darke wordes and not vsuall nor well sounding, though they be dayly spoken in Court.

Daily spoken in court? There we have it. Nobody is exempt from criticism. Everyone—even the queen and the aristocracy—makes mistakes.

So what is the solution? How are things to improve? Puttenham has two suggestions. His first recommendation is perhaps the earliest affirmation of a principle which would become the dominant theme of later centuries: trust the language connoisseurs. If you allow yourself to be ruled, he says, 'by th'English Dictionaries and other bookes written by learnèd men', you will need 'none other direction'.

It's difficult to know what works he was thinking of—perhaps some of the bilingual (e.g. Latin / English) dictionaries—but whatever they were, these books had evidently already acquired some authority, at least in Puttenham's eyes. It was a sign of things to come.

People readily took up Puttenham's first recommendation. Not so his second. Take great care, he advises his poets, that you don't fall into the fault that you condemn in others. If you display a particular fault yourself, then you are 'no meete [suitable] Magistrate to reforme the same errours in any other person'. Rather, if the poet can

> acknowledge his owne fault, and can the better tell how to amend it, he may seeme a more excusable correctour of other mens.

And he concludes: the poet must 'taxe him selfe first and before any others'.

An excellent biblical principle. Sort your own mote out first. If only the self-appointed language watchdogs who followed him had followed that principle, the history of English usage would have been very different. But that, as we shall see, is what self-appointed language watchdogs never do.

8

Rustics

I N 1604, a schoolteacher, Robert Cawdrey, published his *Table Alphabeticall*—an alphabetical list of hard English words and their meanings which has received the accolade of 'the first English dictionary'. In his preface addressed to the reader, he mentions in passing two styles of English, referring to one as 'court talk' and the other as 'country speech'. Court talk, as we have seen in Chapter 7, was 'the best' English. Country speech, by contrast, we must assume was 'the worst'.

And so it was perceived to be, by most of the educated classes. George Puttenham had talked about the 'strange accents' and 'ill-shaped sounds' used by craftsmen and carters and other 'inferior' people. During the sixteenth century, at the same time as the language of the court was increasing in prestige, the language of the countryside was moving steadily in the opposite direction.

Regional accents and dialects had of course been criticized in the Middle Ages, but the criticisms did not reflect any kind of social agenda. Those who disliked regional speech did so either because they did not like the sound of it or because they did not understand it—or both. They did not condemn it because they did not like the people, or thought of them as having unpleasant characteristics. But things changed in the sixteenth century. Regional speech came to be increasingly associated with a set of demeaning social values. And it has been like that ever since.

The stereotypes seem to have started with a genre of publishing that became very popular during the 1500s. Following Caxton's translation of Aesop's *Fables* in 1484, a new type of story-book appeared, illustrated by *A Hundred Mery Talys* ('Merry Tales') in 1526 and *Tales and Quicke Answeres* in 1532. They came to be called 'jest books'—*jest* here having a much broader sense than it has today, including short stories that were entertaining rather than funny. They often involved characters from outside London. Here are four of the titles concerning Welshmen. What image do they convey?

Of the Welshman that confessed him he had slain a friar
Of the Welshman that stole the Englishman's cock
Of the Welshman that shrove him for breaking his fast on the Friday
Of the Welshman that delivered the letter to the ape

Plainly the Welsh are murderers, thieves, sinners, and fools. Nor are they alone. Northerners, Irishmen, and other provincials are also the butt of these tales.

Even if there is nothing in the title, the story nonetheless often contains a stereotype. Here is the tale 'Of them that came to London to buy a crucifix' (I have modernized the spelling):

> There were certain men upon a time sent out of a village to London to buy a crucifix of wood. The courtier that they came to, seeing and hearing by their words that they were but fools, he, blunt fellows, asked them, whether they would have the image alive or else dead. Which question so abashed them, that they went aside to devise whether [which] was best. So when they had spoken privily together, they came to the carver again and said they would have the image alive; for if their neighbours at home were not so content, they might lightly [easily] kill him.

The contrast between the stupid countrymen and the astute Londoner is evidently well established.

There is nothing in the language of these stories that suggests the accent or dialect of the way people spoke. It is guilt by association. The stories present provincial people as naive, simple-minded, ignorant, or untrustworthy, and thus fostered a set of negative attitudes about rural folk which would in due course come to be associated with the way they spoke. The tales provided some cheap laughs, at the expense of regional identity. The best writers never did this.

Chaucer, for instance, is the first English writer to have made characters speak in dialect. *The Reeve's Tale* tells the story of a miller who tries to con two Cambridge university students out of their college's corn. The students are from the north, and they are made to speak in a northern way. But they are not stupid. Far from it: they manage to trick the miller, get their corn, and seduce the miller's wife and daughter into the bargain. It is the southern character which is made to look ridiculous.

Chaucer wasn't lauding northern speech, in this tale, nor was he ridiculing southern speech. Having chosen to make his students northern, and his miller southern, his innovation was simply to write a text which would show the difference. The students are given words and spellings which reflect their background. For example, one of the students wants to see *howgates the corn gas in* ('how the corn goes in'). The *-a-* and the *-s* ending for 'goes' are typically northern. When the miller uses the same word a few lines later, it is spelled in a southern way, *goth* (= 'goeth'). The accents are part of the characters. Chaucer isn't making a point about northern speech sounding more intelligent than southern speech or the other way round. The two accents are just—different. *The Reeve's Tale* is a fine example of dialect democracy.

Nor does Shakespeare ridicule regional dialects as coming from stupid people. The most famous regional speakers in his plays are all well educated. In *Henry V* (III. ii), the Englishman, Irishman, Scotsman, and Welshman each display local dialect features in their speech, but the humour is sympathetic and there is respect for their positions. They are all captains—a senior rank—in Henry's army. If we laugh at the Welshman Fluellen, it is at his explosive temperament and his obsession with military history. Only in the modern era would people come to laugh at him because of the way he speaks.

Shakespeare's rustics abound in the plays, and they are often figures of fun—but never because of anything regional in their speech. Some rustics use as fine language as any Romeo. This is the shepherd Silvius in *As You Like It* (II. iv. 30)

> If thou rememberest not the slightest folly
> That ever love did make thee run into
> Thou hast not loved.

No rustic ever spoke like that. And when we look at Dogberry, Launce, Bottom, and all the other lower-class characters, their language may be colloquial but it is not regional. They could come from any part of the country—and in modern productions, they do. Directors usually add the baggage of a modern regional accent in order to get some easy laughs. The 2005 Royal Shakespeare Company production of *A Midsummer Night's Dream*, for example, gave the mechanicals strong Birmingham accents. For me, it spoiled an otherwise brilliant production. Such events reinforce unpalatable stereotypes that drama, in particular, should be trying to remove.

Shakespeare did not poke fun at native English accents and dialects. His targets for linguistic satire were people who put on linguistic airs and graces, who tried to be what they were not, and who used language as part of the process. Thus we see the pretentiousness of Osric, Holofernes, and Don Armado reflected in their speech. He also pokes fun at people who try to use big words and get them wrong, as with Dogberry, Launcelot Gobbo, and Mistress Quickly.

Foreigners attempting to speak English were fair game too, especially if they were the enemy (as with the French). But regional speech is never a target.

Today, we read in a host of extra values, when we hear someone who is northern or southern, rural or urban, English or Celtic. Why this is so we shall see in a later chapter. But these were not the values in Shakespeare's time. Richard Carew, in *The Excellencie of the English Tongue*, printed in 1614, sums up the contemporary attitude in a single passage. He is proud of the dialect diversity which exists in the country.

> the Copiousnes of our Languadge appeareth in the diuersitye of our dialectes, for wee have court, and we have country English, we have Northern and Southern, gross and ordinary, which differ each from other, not only in the terminations, but also in many words, terms, and phrases, and express the same thinges in diuers sortes, yeat all right Englishe alike.

Yet all [use] right English alike. This must have been Shakespeare's view too.

Nonetheless, during Shakespeare's lifetime, an alternative climate was emerging. Writers were increasingly making cheap jokes at the expense of ordinary folk, and regional speech was becoming implicated. The morality plays and interludes offered particular scope for a contrast between regional and non-regional speech, as they usually presented a confrontation between good and evil, personified by such characters as Vice, Mercy, Ignorance, and Good Deeds. Although one imagines that courtiers as well as rustics could display all these attributes, it was only the bad side of the human character that spoke regionally. In John Redford's *Wit and Science* (probably written in the 1540s, and performed at Henry VIII's court), Idleness asks Ignorance where he was born, and Ignorance replies:

> 'Chwas ibore in Ingland, Mother sed.

'Chwas is *Ich was*, a stage dialect version of the first person pronoun which is widely found in plays at the time, and *ibore* ('born') is another regionalism. Evidently, if you are an ignoramus, you will speak in regional dialect. There is no hint of regionalism in the way Reason, Honest Recreation, and all the other goodies speak.

The foundations of negative stereotypes of regional speech were laid in the sixteenth century, and they became stronger in later centuries, despite the dialect democracy of Shakespeare and some of the other leading writers. In modern times, when people have attempted to halt the process, and restore some respect to regional speech, they have often been condemned for having an outlook that ignored English linguistic tradition. Quite the opposite is the case. The ancient tradition respects regional dialects. It is the puristic trend that is the aberration.

I have often been told off by the linguistically pure-minded for suggesting that regional dialects have a value that is no worse (and of course no better) than we find in standard English. I was once called, in this connection, 'one of these modern liberals'. Me and Shakespeare, both.

9

Authors

Wнo forms the usage climate, in an age lacking grammars, dictionaries, and other linguistic resources? In a word: authors. Literary authors, in the first instance; academic authors, in the second.

In the sixteenth century, the academics actually did very little. As we saw in Chapters 5 and 6, learned writers were preoccupied with rows over spelling and loan words. Hardly anyone bothered to step back and look at the language system as a whole, apart from the occasional work on poetry or rhetoric. Although there were several Latin grammars and Latin dictionaries, there was little activity towards providing equivalents for English.

There was one exception. In the 1580s, the spelling reformer William Bullokar promised a whole 'family' of books in addition to his book on orthography: there were to be a 'sister' book (a grammar) and a 'cousin dictionary'. But he is not happy. He writes at one point that his grammar 'lieth at home, abiding my good chance'—a familiar problem ('I'll get round to it when I have a moment'). We do have an abridged version of this grammar, but the full text—if he ever completed it—is lost. And his proposed dictionary (which 'I know doth lack me much') never appeared. Still, Bullokar's *Pamphlet for Grammar* (1586), even if it is only a sketch, stands as the first English grammar.

The tide would begin to turn in the new century. As already mentioned in the previous chapter, Robert Cawdrey's 'alphabetical table' of hard words was the first proper dictionary, in 1604. It was not very large, containing only 2,449 defined words, and many of the definitions were just brief glosses, but it was nonetheless a breakthrough—the first book to be both alphabetical and definitional, compiled for no other purpose than to explain meaning and usage. His pedagogical aim is quite clear. He has compiled it, he says, 'for the benefit & helpe of Ladies, Gentlewomen, or any other unskilfull persons'. And why?

> Whereby they may the more easilie and better vnderstand many hard English wordes, which they shall heare or read in Scriptures, Sermons, or elswhere, and also be made able to vse the same aptly themselues.

As we would say today: to improve their passive and active vocabulary. Or, as *Reader's Digest* would put it: 'It pays to increase your word power.'

Another grammar was written soon after, by Ben Jonson—known for his plays rather than his linguistics—probably around 1616. But grammar was having bad luck at the time. Not only is Bullokar's complete text lost, but the full text of Jonson's manuscript perished in a fire which destroyed his library in 1623. Only a draft survived, which was published in his collected works in 1640, after his death. Its title is interesting:

> The English Grammar made by B. Jonson for the Benefit of all Strangers out of the Observation of the English Language, now Spoken and in Use.

Unlike Cawdrey's dictionary, this was a grammar for *foreign* learners of English. It was not intended as a guide for native speakers. The first grammars with that end in mind would not appear for another century.

There is something else of interest in Jonson's title: his reference to 'observation'. He relies on extracts from texts to illustrate his grammatical points—the first author to do so. He takes examples from literary writers, such as Chaucer, Gower, and Lydgate, as well as from leading English humanists, such as Thomas More and John Cheke. His description uses the categories of Latin grammar, but the spirit of his work is clear. He quotes the Roman rhetorician Quintilian with approval: '*Custome*, is the most certaine Mistresse of Language, as the publicke stampe makes the current money.' In doing so, he launches one of the major themes in the later history of English usage.

Little guidance about usage from academic writing, then. What of the literary authors? If there is one word which sums up the linguistic state of mind of Spenser, Sidney, Shakespeare, Marlowe, Marston, Nashe, and the other Elizabethan writers, I think it has to be 'resourceful'. They had taken on the task of writing about their own life and times, and the life and times of other countries and periods, and the lives of individuals who, in their imagination and language, were larger than life. Imagine the linguistic character of the English court, of London streets, of ancient Rome, of an Othello. Then find words in Elizabethan English to express it.

Moreover, find words which will also fit the metrical rhythms of the iambic pentameter, the fashionable mode of poetic expression of the time. We can devise a thought experiment to simulate the authors' problem and discover their solution. 'Can this cockpit hold the [INSERT WORD FOR 'LARGE'] fields of France?' asks the Chorus at the beginning of *Henry V*. Shakespeare needs a two-syllable word here. What options were available in the language of the time with the meaning of 'very large'?

There was *large* itself, and *huge*, which had both been in the language since the thirteenth century, and *great*, which had been around since Anglo-Saxon times. But these were common everyday words, not very imaginative—hardly suitable for capturing the enormity of the dramatic scene the Chorus is painting. And in any case, with just one syllable they had the wrong rhythm. *Immense* and *enormous* also existed, but they had the wrong rhythm, too. *Massive* was an option: that had the right rhythm, but unfortunately the wrong meaning. *Massive* expresses the idea of concrete size upwards—as in a *massive building*—not the idea of a flat expanse. *Vast* was the only word which had the right meaning, and was sufficiently unusual to make a poet want to use it. But it too had only one syllable.

There is only one solution, under such circumstances. If there is no word in the language that meets all your needs—semantic, grammatical, phonetic—then you have to invent one. So he did: *vasty*. It feels like a genuine Shakespearian coinage. There are other words like it in the plays—such as *plumpy, brisky, steepy*—and he uses *vasty* on four other occasions. Nobody else is known to have used the word before him.

The Elizabethan period was one of great lexical invention by authors—not just new words but new applications of existing words—that is, new senses. Studies of Shakespeare's vocabulary suggest that he alone coined around 1,700 words, half of which became a permanent part of the language. They include such words as *abstemious* and *accommodation* as well as compounds such as *well-ordered* and *well-read*. Some of them are mundane (*outgrow, unhelpful*); some are highly inventive (*intertissued, languageless*). But all illustrate a readiness to coin, and to exploit the existing resources of the language in order to do so.

Everyone coined and adapted. It was the natural thing to do. The *Oxford English Dictionary* records tell us that some 800 new words are attributed to Thomas Nashe, 500 to Spenser, and 400 to Sidney, and several other authors have significant numbers too. With no centralized means of recording usage, of course, the only way one author would know what others were doing was by the slow process of serendipitous encounter—in the playhouse, in a quarto text, in a tavern. And even then, you might only notice the more dramatic coinages. As a result, faced with a need for a new word, individuals would be as likely to coin anew as to copy existing usage.

We can see this happening in the multiplicity of new word-forms coined to express the same concept. The notion of being 'characterized by discord', for example, generated *discordous*, *discording*, *discordant*, and *discordful*, each used by a different writer. *Discordant* eventually entered the language; the others died away. Why did that one survive? Shakespeare was the one who used it, though he did not invent it—the word is known in Middle English. Was it his usage which made the word well known? Or were there some other factors? Why some coinages enter the language and some don't is one of the great mysteries of English linguistic history.

You might think that everyone would be delighted to see such a flowering of linguistic creativity. And indeed, in the annals of dramatic criticism, with just occasional exceptions, the lexical inventiveness of the Elizabethan and Jacobean dramatists is a source of great admiration. But outside the theatrical world, there were murmurs of discontent. If writers invented words whenever they wanted to, this was a road pointing towards chaos. The language, many felt, was out of control. It needed to be reined in. The mood took a while to grow, but during the 1600s these murmurs turned into growls.

10

Censurers

WHO thought the language was out of control, in the seventeenth century? Most of the social elite, judging by the essays and proposals which have come down to us. When the Royal Society was established in London, in 1660, the issue of language was one of the first to be addressed.

In 1667, Thomas Sprat wrote a history of the Society in which he censured the philosophy of the 'school-men' of an earlier age. But he doesn't restrict himself to a criticism of what they were saying; he has harsh things to say about how they were saying it. Note especially, he says, 'the Barbarousness of their style' and their 'want of good Language'.

What exactly was Sprat thinking of? Chiefly, what he called their ornateness and eloquence. We might think that these were positive qualities of usage, not negative ones—but this is not the way he takes them. He—and he aligns the whole Society with him—is against what he calls 'the luxury and redundance of speech'. People, quite simply, have been talking too much. He goes on:

> The ill effects of this superfluity of talking, have already over-whelm'd most other *Arts* and *Professions*.

and he does not want the same thing to happen to the sciences. But it is not just science that is affected:

> *eloquence* ought to be banish'd out of all *civil Societies*, as a thing fatal to Peace and good Manners.

A proper scientific approach, he suggests, needs to avoid rhetoric, metaphors, and classical vocabulary, which get in the way of clear thinking.

> Who can behold, without indignation, how many mists and uncertainties, these specious *Tropes* and *Figures* have brought on our Knowledg? How many rewards, which are due to more profitable, and difficult *Arts*, have been still snatch'd away by the easie vanity of *fine speaking*? For now I am warm'd with this just Anger, I cannot with-hold myself, from betraying the shallowness of all these seeming Mysteries; upon which, *we Writers*, and *Speakers*, look so bigg. And, in few words, I dare say; that of all the Studies of men, nothing may be sooner obtain'd, than their vicious abundance of *Phrase*, this trick of *Metaphors*, this volubility of *Tongue*, which makes so great a noise in the World.

Without indignation. Just anger. Vicious, trick, noise… The arguments are growing increasingly intemperate. It isn't 'disgusted of Tunbridge Wells', quite, but it is close: the writer would become Bishop of Rochester in 1684.

Sprat is one of the first to say, quite plainly, that the English language has been deteriorating and is continuing to do so. And, as with all who would make the same assertion in later generations, he sees the problem as symptomatic of more general social evils, especially wars and the decline of religious practice. The decay in language, he says,

> may be plac'd amongst those *general mischiefs*; such, as the *dissention* of Christian Princes, the *want of practice* in Religion, and the like.

The italics well capture his mood; they were used at the time to signal words a writer felt to be important. Sprat was writing, we must recall, soon after the end of twenty years of civil war in Britain, and at the end of a period which has been described by one historian, Paul Slack, as an age of 'obvious instability'. He comments:

> people at the end of the period saw themselves in a society beset with uncertainties and continuous flux, and they spent a good deal of time proclaiming the virtues of 'order' and 'degree' against dangers which seemed to lurk all around.

Sprat is clear about what needs to be done, to prevent the language from going completely downhill. The 'only remedy', he says, is to avoid the extravagances of the past, which is what he hopes the Royal Society will do:

> to reject all the amplifications, digressions, and swellings of style: to return back to the primitive purity, and shortness, when men deliver'd so many *things*, almost in an equal number of *words*.

What we want, he says, is

> a close, naked, natural way of speaking; positive expressions; clear senses...

And where are these to be found?

> preferring the language of Artizans, Countrymen, and Merchants, before that, of Wits, or Scholars.

What a turnaround from Puttenham's day (Chapter 7), when the last place you would look for guidance about usage was in the speech of 'merchants and travellers'.

But it was all a romantic pipe-dream. Primitive purity? Sprat's own discourse was full of the very language he was complaining about. His metaphors talk about English being in need of 'cure'; a desirable way of speaking should be 'naked'. His sentences rely on classical vocabulary and swelling style. And not by any stretch of the imagination could his elegantly balanced and complex paragraphs be described as a 'natural way of speaking'. The language of merchants is fascinating and complex in its own way, but we all know it is not like this. And, notwithstanding his protests, Royal Society publications in due course took their place within the general tradition of ornate academic writing.

Sprat's heart is in the right place. Everyone would agree that it is desirable for language to be clear. The problem is in saying clearly what constitutes this clarity, and this is what Sprat is unable to do. We can hardly blame him. No one has ever been able to define the linguistic basis of such notions as clarity, simplicity, and elegance. We can usually recognize such qualities when we see or hear them; but *define* them? A century later, grammarians tried again, thinking that the solution lay in a small set of grammatical rules. That didn't work either.

There is no simple relationship between clarity and language. Apart from a few well-known exceptions, such as in poetry and politics ('Now let me be absolutely clear about this...'), everyone wants to be clear, and everyone admires clarity of expression in others. But clarity cannot be achieved by forbidding the use of whole areas of language, such as figures of speech or classical vocabulary, for the obvious reason that a thought might be best expressed by using precisely those means. Even science makes copious use of metaphors: witness the 'flavours' of quarks in particle physics, or the 'blind watchmaker' of evolutionary biology.

Clarity depends on our making judicious use of *all* of a language's resources. Words, grammar, rhythm, discourse, and stylistic level all play their part. It is never possible to identify a single dimension or principle of usage, or a cluster of 'rules', and say that these are obligatory features of clarity of expression. When people try to do this, they invariably end up—as did Sprat—breaking the very principles they have themselves promulgated. We shall see this happening repeatedly, as criticisms of usage grow.

Sprat is sweeping in his condemnation of scholarly language of a previous age. So, a few years later, was John Dryden, though his target was the language of literature. Dryden wrote an essay in 1672 called 'In Defence of the Epilogue'—a reference to a verse epilogue that he had written for his play *The Conquest of Granada*. This is what he has to say about Shakespeare's and Jonson's 'Sence and Language':

> I dare almost challenge any man to show me a page together, which is correct in both.

What exactly was Dryden thinking of? What are the errors that can be found on every page of Jonson and Shakespeare? He gives several examples from Jonson. One is the use of the 'double comparative' construction, illustrated by *Contain your Spirit in more stricter bounds*. He calls this 'gross'. In fact, it was a perfectly normal grammatical construction in Elizabethan English, used by everyone. It was falling out of use in Dryden's day, and would eventually leave standard English altogether. Today, locutions such as *more bigger*, as an emphatic kind of comparison, will be found only in regional dialects. They are rigorously excluded from standard English.

All dialects are defined partly by the rules of grammar they employ. If speakers of modern standard English have decided (either unconsciously or by following a grammarian's diktat) that double comparatives are unacceptable, then we have to respect that. But we have to give the same respect to other dialects that have made a different decision about the matter. And we certainly should not be judging the standards of the past by the standards of the present. Historians have a word for this: presentism. Dryden was an early linguistic presentist.

But at least Jonson was learnèd, and someone Dryden greatly admired. As for people with less learning, what hope for them?

And what correctness after this, can be expected from Shakespear or from Fletcher, who wanted [lacked] that Learning and Care which Johnson had? I will therefore spare my own trouble of inquiring into their faults: who had they liv'd now, had doubtless written more correctly.

Doubtless, if Shakespeare had lived now, he would have written more correctly. This sums up a growing mindset about usage as the eighteenth century drew near.

II

Protectors

John Dryden had a solution to the problem of a deteriorating language. The Royal Society had set up a committee in December 1664 'for improving the English language', and he was a member. At a series of meetings in Gray's Inn, they explored the idea of founding an institution to look after English. An Academy.

An Academy had been founded in France thirty years before, so there was already a model. Another committee member, the polymath John Evelyn, enthusiastically proposed that an English Academy could carry out similar activities. There could be a grammar and a dictionary, collections of dialect words, guides to spelling reform, translations to act as models of excellence...

Nothing happened. The meetings ended early the following year. We do not know why. Perhaps the other Society members were not as enthusiastic as Evelyn and Dryden. Perhaps they realized just how huge and costly an undertaking such an enterprise would be. Or perhaps it was simply that other events overtook them. The arrival of bubonic plague in the spring of 1665 would have hampered ongoing debate, for everyone who could leave

London did so. And a year later there was a Great Fire to contend with.

But the idea of an Academy did not go away. Wentworth Dillon, the Earl of Roscommon, took up the idea in the 1680s, according to Samuel Johnson, who edited an edition of his works. Impressed by the foreign academies, Roscommon 'formed the plan of a society for refining our language, and fixing its standard'. Dryden is said to have helped him. But once again, the idea sinks without trace. The short and turbulent reign of James II was not a good time to be looking for national support for a language project.

Daniel Defoe was the next to run with the idea. He develops it at length in a well-known article written in 1697: 'On Academies'. It is a specific proposal that the king—William III now—should establish a society 'to polish and refine the English Tongue'. But there is more, much more. The society would also

> advance the so much neglected Faculty of Correct Language, to establish Purity and Propriety of Stile, and to purge it from all the Irregular Additions that Ignorance and Affectation have introduc'd; and all those Innovations in Speech, if I may call them such, which some Dogmatic Writers have the Confidence to foster upon their Native Language, as if their Authority were sufficient to make their own Fancy legitimate.

The terminology of excellence is much increased, in these lines. It is no longer a simple matter of clarity: the language needs to have purity and propriety, and all irregularities and innovations have to be purged. And one of the chief aims of such an Academy would be to eliminate what he calls 'that Scum and Excrement of the Mouth... a mere Frenzy of the Tongue, a Vomit of the Brain'—namely, swearing. Almost half his essay is an attack on bad language, which would be discouraged, he hopes, by the example of academicians.

And who would be these clean-mouthed academicians? Who would be authorized to stand in judgment about language matters? We want learned people, certainly, says Defoe, but not those whose business is learning. Certainly no academics!

> We have seen many great Scholars, meer Learned Men, and Graduates in the last Degree of Study, whose English has been far from Polite, full of Stiffness and Affectation, hard Words, and long unusual Coupling of Syllables and Sentences, which sound harsh and untuneable to the Ear, and shock the Reader both in Expression and Understanding.
>
> In short, There should be room in this Society for neither Clergyman, Physician, or Lawyer...

So who is left?

> I wou'd therefore have this Society wholly compos'd of Gentlemen; whereof Twelve to be of the Nobility, if possible, and Twelve Private Gentlemen, and a Class of Twelve to be left open for meer merit.

Defoe believed that his Academy would have such a reputation that people would readily acknowledge its members to be 'the allow'd Judges of Stile and Language'. Authors, he thought, would not have 'the Impudence to Coin without their Authority'. Indeed, 'twou'd be as Criminal then to Coin Words, as Money.

This is the earliest mention I have encountered, in this context, of an association between bad usage and crime. Defoe would doubtless be the patron saint of zero tolerance.

Once again, the idea came to nothing. The king's attention was taken up with European wars, conflicts between Whigs and Tories, and assassination plots. English language proposals were the least of a Dutch Stuart king's worries.

And so we reach 1712, and Jonathan Swift's 'Proposal for Correcting, Improving and Ascertaining the English Tongue'. The work, he says, needs the protection of a prince, and he hopes the first minister, Robert Harley, Earl of Oxford, will provide it. Our language, he maintains,

> is extremely imperfect;… its daily Improvements are by no means in proportion to its daily Corruptions;… it offends against every Part of Grammar.

Who was to blame for these corruptions? Swift is in no doubt: virtually anyone who writes anything. And he lists them all:

- the playwrights, who fill their works 'with a Succession of affected Phrases, and new, conceited Words';
- the poets, who 'have contributed very much to the spoiling of the English tongue';
- the reformers, who think 'we ought to spell exactly as we speak';
- the young academics, who 'come up to Town, reckon all their Errors for Accomplishments, borrow the newest Sett

of Phrases, and if they take Pen into their Hands, all the odd words they have picked up in a Coffee-House or a Gaming Ordinary [gambling-house], are produced as Flowers of Style'.

What was Swift thinking of, when he talked about the poets spoiling English? He was remembering their 'barbarous Custom of abbreviating Words, to fit them to the Measure of their Verses'. He is thinking of cases like *drudg'd*, *disturb'd*, and *rebuk't*, in prose as well as verse—a practice which forms 'such harsh unharmonious Sounds, that none but a Northern Ear could endure'. And he adds: 'most of the Books we see now a-days, are full of those Manglings and Abbreviations'.

It is a curious criticism, as there was no difference in pronunciation at the time—any more than there is now— between *disturbed* and *disturb'd*. The contrast is purely visual. But it is an interesting criticism, especially if we glance back at the quotations from Defoe and Dryden. Defoe regularly uses the apostrophe: *wou'd*, *compos'd*, *introduc'd*. So he is a barbarian. Even more so is Dryden: in the opening paragraph of his essay we find *oblig'd*, *ingag'd*, *tax'd*, *excell'd*, and *propos'd*. Barbarians all.

It seems to be one of the consequences of becoming a usage critic that your own usage will be pilloried sooner or later. Dryden and Defoe castigate the usage of Jonson and Shakespeare. Swift castigates the usage of Dryden and Defoe. And in due course, as we shall see, eighteenth-century prescriptive grammarians castigate Swift for carelessness.

Then those grammarians begin to criticize each other, as they continue to do today.

Swift's proposal fared no better than those of his predecessors. The Tory ministry fell in 1714, and with it the Earl of Oxford. Harley was dismissed, and after the accession of George I he was impeached and spent two years in prison. In the view of another aristocrat, Lord Chesterfield, this was a blessing in disguise. He did not think it a good idea for politicians to be involved in Academies—'precision and perspicuity not being in general the favourite objects of ministers...'. And he sticks the knife in: '... and perhaps still less of that minister than of any other'.

It was Dr Johnson who, with characteristic good sense, saw the flaw in the English Academy movement. The French Academy hasn't succeeded in 'fixing' their language, he observes; and if the French were unable to do it, with their absolutist government, what chance will an Academy have faced with the bolshy, democratic British temperament?

> We live in an age in which it is a kind of publick sport to refuse all respect that cannot be enforced. The edicts of an English academy would probably be read by many, only that they might be sure to disobey them.

And he concludes:

> That our language is in perpetual danger of corruption cannot be denied; but what prevention can be found? The present manners of the nation would deride authority, and therefore nothing is left but that every writer should criticise himself.

Johnson was writing in 1779. The suggestion that 'every writer should criticise himself' was an excellent one—would that it happened today!—but it was really not an option in the seventeenth and eighteenth centuries. That way could only lead to anarchy. Swift has serious doubts about putting power into the hands of Everyman. 'I am afraid', he says at one point in his Proposal, 'we are naturally not very Polite.' Left to themselves, people will descend into barbarism.

And so, with all proposals for an Academy having come to nothing, and with the motivation and judgement of individuals suspect, where else could guidance about usage come from? There had to be authorities to save the language from chaos.

12

Chaos

PHILIP Stanhope, Lord Chesterfield, has been mentioned. In November 1754, in a letter to *The World* periodical, he sums up the linguistic mood of the time:

> It must be owned that our language is at present in a state of anarchy.

And Samuel Johnson concurred. His *Dictionary* would be published the following year, after several years of exhausting compilation. He writes in the preface:

> When I took the first survey of my undertaking, I found our speech copious without order, and energetick without rules: wherever I turned my view, there was perplexity to be disentangled, and confusion to be regulated; choice was to be made out of boundless variety, without any established principle of selection.

It wasn't just the uncontrolled innovation of previous literary ages which caused this sense of chaos. Something much more fundamental was taking place. The population of England had doubled between 1550 and 1650, reaching 5 million. It was 6 million by 1700. Not only was London the largest city by population in Western Europe (575,000 in 1700), but new cities were rapidly growing all over the country. New social networks came into being, as a result of the population growth, and in due course the language reflects it. *Ghetto* is first recorded in 1611; *suburban* in 1625.

The linguistic consequence was a new sense of regional variation. We have already seen how accents and dialects were sidelined in the sixteenth century, the butt of jokes. The only people to take them seriously were a few antiquarians. But now they were back, with a vengeance. Here, too, the language keeps pace. The terms *accent* and *dialect* arrive. *Dialect* emerges in the 1570s, referring to the way a group of people use vocabulary and grammar in a local way. And Shakespeare is the first recorded user of *accent* (in the sense of a group's manner of pronunciation) when Orlando comments on disguised Rosalind's 'accent' in *As You Like It* (III. ii. 328). In the mid-seventeenth century we find *vernacular*, in the sense of a local variety, as well as a number of contemptuous terms, such as *lingo*, *patois*, and *cant*—this last a musical term applied to the whining speech of beggars.

Accents and dialects exist to give a vocal identity to regional and social communities. They are particularly valuable in this connection because the voice is natural, cheap, and noticeable. We might use distinctive clothing or ornaments to show where we come from, but these can be costly, and they are not always perceptible—such as around corners or in the dark. The voice avoids these limitations.

Accents and dialects are both inward-looking, fostering group solidarity, and outward-looking, fostering group distance. 'We are like us, and we are not like them.' The more speakers there are, of course, and the more they encounter each other, the more the distinctive features of an accent or dialect become noticed, imitated, exaggerated, and satirized. And in the eighteenth century, there were significantly more people than before, and they travelled more often. Improved roads and methods of transportation reduced travel times and increased the number of journeys. There were thirty coaches a day travelling between London and Birmingham in the 1760s. In 1740 there had been just one.

Britain had never seen such an increase in the numbers of regional speakers as took place in the seventeenth and eighteenth centuries. We might interpret this as a sign of linguistic vitality. But what one person sees as an enriching diversity, another person sees as a divisive fragmentation. To the observers of the time, such as Swift and Chesterfield, this was further evidence that the language was headed for disaster.

It was not just the increase in regional speakers which worried them; it was the change in their social character. These were not rustics. They were businessmen, merchants, and industrialists, an increasingly powerful sector of society, whose numbers would be further swelled as the Industrial Revolution progressed. They were an increasingly literate section of society, too: by 1700 nearly half of the male population and a quarter of the female population of England were able to read and write.

And they were an increasingly genteel section of society. The growth of the gentry, a class below the peerage, had been one of the most important developments of the late Middle Ages, and it became a major feature of seventeenth- and eighteenth-century life. It was a very broad and disparate group, chiefly including anyone who had an income derived from land that was physically worked by others. Such people usually had local government responsibilities—for example, acting as magistrates. They and their sons would probably have spent time at a university or one of the Inns of Court.

And how were you to behave, if you had become a member of this new class of gentry? Books of etiquette, conduct guides, and courtesy manuals came to be written, defining gentility. One influential book was by George Savile, Lord Halifax, who wrote *Lady's New Year's Gift; or, Advice to a Daughter* (1688). All aspects of behaviour had to be dealt with—how to bow, shake hands, wear a hat, hold gloves, eat with a fork, pour tea, use a napkin, or blow your nose in public. Also, what not to do: no spitting, chewing with the mouth open, eating with your hands.

In one of Lord Chesterfield's *Letters to his Son* (19 March 1750) we first encounter the word *etiquette* in English, and he does not beat about the bush. In that same letter we read:

> For instance: do you use yourself to carve, eat, and drink
> genteelly, and with ease? Do you take care to walk, sit, stand,
> and present yourself gracefully? Are you sufficiently upon
> your guard against awkward attitudes, and illiberal, ill-bred,
> and disgusting habits; such as scratching yourself, putting your
> fingers in your mouth, nose, and ears? Tricks always acquired

at schools, often too much neglected afterwards; but, however, extremely ill-bred and nauseous.

Worries about language keep company with worries about manners. It would be the same in the 2000s, with *Eats, Shoots and Leaves* morphing into *Talk to the Hand*.

There are several words which capture the spirit of the age—'polish', 'refinement', 'propriety', and 'manners'; but the most important watchword for behaviour was 'politeness', recorded in this sense in 1702 (though the adjective, *polite*, was several decades earlier). Swift had described his century as 'this Age of Learning and Politeness'. Dr Johnson's definition of *politeness* was 'elegance of manners; gentility; good breeding'. And 'polite language' was thought to be a use of English which was widely intelligible and acceptable— polished, elegant, correct.

It was the correctness which was the ultimate guarantor of its politeness. This word in its application to language had come into English towards the end of the seventeenth century. Gilbert Burnet comments in the preface to his 1684 translation of Sir Thomas More's *Utopia* about 'the fidelity of the Translation, and the correctness of the English'. The speed with which this notion of 'correct English' was taken up, promulgated, and institutionalized during the eighteenth century is one of the most remarkable developments in the history of the language.

Evidently the notion was too important to continue being left to the uncontrolled intuitions of literary authors and enthusiastic amateurs. Important as these may have been in the compilation of early manuals and in the formation of attitudes towards the distinction between standard and non-standard, it seems that people now felt the need for more authoritative custodians, if the language was to progress. Accordingly, as we leave the Early Modern English period, we enter the age of the authorities.

13

Authorities

'Every polite tongue has its own rules,' asserted the grammarian Lindley Murray. And it was the job of the grammarians, lexicographers, pronunciation analysts, and stylists to make sure that these rules were known, appreciated, and followed. The polite people themselves could not help; for it was precisely that section of society which was perpetually getting them wrong.

In tracing attitudes to English usage during the eighteenth century, there is nothing more important than to understand the mindset of those who set themselves up as language authorities, for this would colour our entire way of thinking for the next 300 years. Indeed, it is only in the latter part of the twentieth century that we have begun to free ourselves from it, and started to give language realities the sort of recognition which was routine in earlier ages.

The mindset can be summarized in four steps:

- Left to themselves, polite people do not speak or write correctly.
- Grammars, dictionaries, and other manuals are therefore needed in order to instruct polite society in the correct ways of speaking and writing.

- No one is exempt. Even the best authors, such as Shakespeare, break the rules from time to time.
- And if even Shakespeare breaks the rules, this proves the need for guidance, because lesser mortals are even more likely to fall into the same trap.

Exactly the same argument was being used in the twentieth century, except that for 'polite' read 'educated'.

If authorities are needed to write the manuals of instruction, two questions immediately arise. Whose English will provide the standard of correctness? And who will come forward to act as an authority in such matters?

The speech of the court provided an obvious answer to the first question, just as it had done in previous centuries. The term 'King's English' had come to the fore some 200 years earlier, being first recorded in 1553. It became the 'Queen's English' a few years later. And responsibility varied between kings and queens thereafter, along with their court, which according to Swift was 'the Standard of Propriety and Correctness of Speech'. Or rather, it should have been, for Swift by no means approved of the 'licentiousness' of the Restoration court, and the language of its members he felt left a great deal to be desired.

If royalty was letting us down, then what about religion? Swift noted that the Bible and the Book of Common Prayer held a special place:

> For those Books being perpetually read in Churches, have proved a kind of Standard for language, especially to the common People.

And the grammarians Lowth and Murray (Chapter 17) later agreed:

> The present translation of the Bible is the best standard of the English language.

However, this source of possible correctness was becoming suspect too. Puritanism and the other religious movements of the age had brought competing translations and terms, and—as we saw in Chapter 6—increasing controversy. If people would take Tyndale to task for minor matters of punctuation, what hope was there in religious sources for the notion of correctness?

A third possibility sounded more promising. The dictionaries. Dictionary compilation was a genre that had grown enormously since Cawdrey's first effort in 1604. John Kersey had compiled a dictionary in 1702 with 28,000 words. Nathan Bailey had compiled another, in 1721, and this had grown to 60,000 words by its 1736 edition. But to Lord Chesterfield, these were of little help. He dismisses them as mere 'word-books', in which 'all words, good and bad, are there jumbled indiscriminately together'.

What Chesterfield wants is a real authority, someone he can trust to guide him through the minefields of usage. It's a disgrace, he says, that our nation has no such standard:

> The time for discrimination seems to be now come. Toleration, adoption and naturalization have run their lengths. Good order and authority are now necessary.

Bailey and the others, competent though they were, were simply not authoritative enough, in his view. They were certainly fuller in their accounts, compared with the earlier books of hard words, but their entries did not contain examples of the way prestigious authors used the language, and they gave no guidance about usage. It wasn't enough to have a lexicographer's say-so. There had to be evidence.

In any case, the lexicographers had been disagreeing amongst themselves. In the middle of the seventeenth century, there had been a furious row between two of them. The lawyer Thomas Blount had compiled a *Glossographia* of hard words in 1656. Two years later, Edward Phillips—the nephew of John Milton—published *The New World of Words*. Then in 1673 there was a riposte from Blount: *A World of Errors Discovered in the New World of Words*—accusing him of including 'barbarous and illegally compounded words'. Phillips replied in like terms. This was not the only occasion that lexicographers fell out. No wonder Lord Chesterfield was looking for authority.

Enter Samuel Johnson, who was looking for a sponsor. In 1747 Johnson wrote a Plan for his huge *Dictionary* project, and sent it to Chesterfield. It seemed to be right up his lordship's street. Johnson proposed to 'fix' the language:

> This, my Lord, is my idea of an English dictionary, a diction-
> ary by which the pronunciation of our language may be fixed,
> and its attainment facilitated; by which its purity may be
> preserved, its use ascertained, and its duration lengthened.

We might have expected Chesterfield to fall over himself to give Johnson his support—and his money. But Johnson got no reply. And when Chesterfield did eventually praise Johnson's work, seven years later, Johnson sent him one of the loftiest put-downs in English literary history.

> Is not a Patron, my Lord, one who looks with unconcern on a man struggling for life in the water, and, when he has reached ground, encumbers him with help? The notice which you have been pleased to take of my labours, had it been early, had been kind; but it has been delayed till I am indifferent, and cannot enjoy it; till I am solitary, and cannot impart it; till I am known and do not want it.

And in his dictionary, we find the first sense of *patron* as follows:

> One who countenances, supports or protects. Commonly a wretch who supports with insolence, and is paid with flattery.

If anyone had the personality with the stamp of 'authority' all over it, in the eighteenth century, it was Johnson. But Johnson was careful to stand on as many prestigious shoulders as he could. His dictionary is innovative chiefly in the way he includes quotations—over 200,000 of them— to substantiate his definitions. Half of them come from just seven sources: Shakespeare, Dryden, Milton, Addison, Bacon, Pope, and the Bible. As he says in his preface:

> I have studiously endeavoured to collect examples and authorities from the writers before the restoration, whose works I regard as the wells of English undefiled, as the pure sources of genuine diction.

The *Dictionary* would itself be criticized in due course for unevenness. Several of the words Johnson included—such as *incompossibility* and *morbifical*—seem to be there more for their Latinate impressiveness than for their relevance to English. But when the book appeared, in 1755, its authoritativeness was second to none.

Chesterfield himself was in no doubt. In a remarkable statement, he illustrates the mindset of his age. We must choose a 'dictator', he says, to provide order in the language, and:

> I give my vote for Mr Johnson to fill that great and arduous post. And I hereby declare that I make a total surrender of all my rights and privileges in the English language, as a freeborn British subject, to the said Mr Johnson, during the term of his dictatorship. Nay more; I will not only obey him, like an old Roman, as my dictator, but, like a modern Roman, I will implicitly believe in him as my pope, and hold him to be infallible while in the chair; but no longer.

Dictators? Popes? Infallibility? This is extreme language, but it is by no means unusual, either then or since. However, it did raise a few eyebrows. On the other side of the Atlantic, it raised the lexicographer Noah Webster's (Chapter 24). He looks at Britain, but can't believe what he sees. In his influential *Dissertations on the English Language* (1789) he writes:

> strange as it may seem, even well-bred people and scholars, often surrender their right of private judgement to these literary governors. The *ipse dixit* [he—the Master—said it] of

a Johnson, a Garrick, or a Sheridan, has the force of law, and to contradict it is rebellion.

Strange it is indeed. People who would never dream of allowing themselves to be ordered around in other walks of life are prepared to bow meekly when a language expert speaks.

14

Change

J OHNSON was the first widely acknowledged linguistic authority of the eighteenth century. His dictionary dominated lexicography for the next 125 years. Only when the big Oxford project got under way in the last quarter of the nineteenth century did the situation alter—and even then the editors bowed in Johnson's direction when they named it *The New English Dictionary* (the forerunner of The *Oxford English Dictionary*).

Johnson did not shirk from giving his opinions about many of the words he included in his dictionary. *Budge*, he says, is 'a low word'; *dissunder* is 'a barbarous word'. In the *Rambler* periodical for 1752 he says:

> I have laboured to refine our language to grammatical purity, and to clear it from colloquial barbarisms, licentious idioms, and irregular combinations.

Elsewhere, as we have seen, he hoped to 'fix' the language—to stabilize it, make it secure against change.

His social aim was understandable, given the climate of the time. He wanted to warn his peers, who had to survive in a climate of politeness, which words would be judged acceptable in society and which would not. His terminology is more personal and judgemental than we are used to today, but it is not that far away in intention from that used by modern lexicographers, who assign to words such labels as 'formal', 'colloquial', 'pejorative', and 'taboo'.

However, in relation to 'fixing' the language, his dictionary work soon taught him the error of his ways. He recants, in a famous passage in the preface to the *Dictionary*:

> When we see men grow old and die at a certain time one after another, from century to century, we laugh at the elixir that promises to prolong life to a thousand years; and with equal justice may the lexicographer be derided, who being able to produce no example of a nation that has preserved their words and phrases from mutability, shall imagine that his dictionary can embalm his language, and secure it from corruption and decay, that it is in his power to change sublunary nature, and clear the world at once from folly, vanity, and affectation.

This is a lesson everyone who studies language eventually learns. You cannot stop language change. You may not like it; you may regret the arrival of new forms and the passing of old ones; but there is not the slightest thing you can do about it. Language change is as natural as breathing. It is one of the linguistic facts of life.

There is not the slightest thing we can do about it? Actually, there is one thing. We can learn to understand it, come to terms with it, and thus manage it. If all the energy that has been fruitlessly spent over the past 300 years complaining about language change had been devoted to improving our grasp of the nature of language, and developing fresh methods of language teaching and learning, we would all be a lot better off. This is, in fact, the business of that branch of linguistics called 'historical linguistics'—a subject that has yet to receive the wider public recognition that it deserves.

Studying language change is important because it gives us unique insight into human society and identity. I do not use the word 'unique' lightly. What other way is there of understanding an earlier period of social history except through the language in which the people expressed themselves? That language, in its words, grammar, and patterns of discourse—sometimes even in its pronunciation, spelling, and punctuation—reflects the realities of their time. That is what adds interest to such words as *powdering-tub* in Shakespeare or *aleconner* in Johnson. The former: a hot bath for the treatment of venereal diseases. The latter: an officer in the city of London whose job was to inspect the measures given out in public houses.

There is also a practical, everyday reason for studying language change. We need to be aware of the areas in the language that are in the process of changing, so that we can be alert to the possibilities of misunderstanding. There are always several words in the language whose meaning is shifting. If one person is using *refute* to mean *deny* and another person is not, then the risk of ambiguity is present. Such issues need to be part of language-awareness training in schools and courses. It is not enough just to condemn a new usage as incorrect and expect the problem to go away. It won't.

To study language without reference to change is to place it in a social vacuum. Language cannot exist without people. To study language change is to study people change. The only languages that do not change are dead ones.

And change means variation. Language change is not a single thing, which happens overnight, across the board. It is a fashion, which takes time to catch on. One section of society introduces a change, and others slowly pick it up. Women may use it more than men. Young people more than old. One region more than another. One class more than another. Eventually the change takes hold and everyone uses it. Or it doesn't take hold, and just some sections of society end up using it. Either way, the result is variation: different words, grammatical constructions, pronunciations, or spellings being used by different groups of people at the same time. In a word: diversity.

Johnson was one of the first to see this, and it is one of the mysteries of the history of English usage that this side of his thinking did not become as influential as his other side. The side that everyone remembers is his pontificating. But he was also very much concerned about diversity. One of his most famous remarks, which gets into all the quotation books, concerns linguistic diversity:

> I am always sorry when any language is lost, because languages are the pedigree of nations.

For 'languages', read also 'dialects', 'varieties', 'styles'. Concerned as Johnson was to promote a standard language, he did not wish this to be at the expense of other kinds of usage. There is a nice moment when he harangues poor Boswell, who writes:

> I passed an evening with him at his house. He advised me to complete a Dictionary of words peculiar to Scotland, of which I showed him a specimen. 'Sir,' said he, 'Ray has made a collection of north country words. By collecting those of your country, you will do a useful thing towards the history of the language.' He bade me also go on with collections which I was making upon the antiquities of Scotland. 'Make a large book—a folio.' BOSWELL: 'But of what use will it be, sir?' JOHNSON: 'Never mind the use; do it.'

Johnson reflected the climate of his time in calling change 'corruption and decay', and that has been the dominant idiom since. But surely it is time to rid ourselves of the mindset reflected in that phraseology? It makes no sense. When Dryden and Defoe wrote in similar terms it was over 300 years ago. They moaned about corruption and decay, yet here is Johnson, almost a century later, using the English language in his essays as effectively as anyone can imagine. Johnson nevertheless moaned about corruption and decay, yet a century later we find Charles Dickens using the language as effectively as anyone can imagine. Others then, as we shall see, moaned about corruption and decay. A century later we find *N*—you insert the name of your favourite modern novelist, poet, or dramatist—using the language as effectively as anyone can imagine. Today, some people still moan about corruption and decay. And a century later...?

Plainly the idiom of 'corruption and decay' is—to quote the 2006 BBC television series on English etymology—balderdash and piffle. What is happening here is change, change, change, but the language is not getting worse as the result of it. Nor is it getting better. It is just—changing. It is keeping pace with society, as it always must, sometimes changing slowly, sometimes rapidly. Today, with so much social change about, especially as the result of increasing ethnic diversity, the spread of English as a global language, and the effect of Internet technology, we find the language changing more rapidly and widely than ever before.

This puts some people in a real panic. They see a disaster scenario. But there is no need. If the language had been decaying at the rate of knots predicted by Dryden *et al.*, there would have been no language left by now!

15

Grammar

S INCE the 1930s, the approach to usage which typifies the eighteenth century has been called *prescriptive*. It is a word which doesn't appear in Johnson's *Dictionary*, presumably because it was just arriving in English at the time, and it escaped his net. Certainly he used it himself several times in later years. It seems to have had mainly a legal and political force, but in an edition of the *Trifler* periodical in 1788 we see another sense emerging:

Prescriptive rules for the preservation of health.

Prescriptive rules tell you to do things. The medical sense of the noun *prescription* is of course the everyday sense today. We get prescriptions from doctors because we are unwell, and we hope their recommendations will make us better.

To many people in the middle decades of the eighteenth century, the language was indeed seriously unwell. It was suffering from a raging disease of uncontrolled usage. And it needed professional help if it was to get better. The interesting thing is that people still felt this even after the publication of Johnson's *Dictionary*. Why? Why, if he was so authoritative, was this work not enough?

Because a dictionary has limitations. It is not the whole of a language. In fact, in many ways it deals with the least important part, when the question arises of how to create a standard language. This is because the contentious words within the vocabulary of a language—the words which are borrowed from other languages or which are changing their usage in some way—simply do not turn up very often.

Think of a clutch of words which are contentious today, and ask how often you are likely to see them on any page of this book (apart from the present one) or, for that matter, in any other: *refute*, *disinterested*, *decimate*, *biennial*, *mitigate*, *infer*... They are all uncommon. And that makes them of limited value when it comes to identifying standard usage. It isn't much help if we have to wait half an hour for someone to use one of these words before we know whether they are speaking standard English or not.

There was an urgency surrounding the notion of a standard language, in the eighteenth century. People needed to know who they were talking to. Snap judgements were everything, when it came to social position. And things are not much different today. We make immediate judgements based on how people dress, how they do their hair, decorate their bodies—and how they speak and write. It is the first bit of discourse that counts.

So, if it is important for us to know whether someone is speaking or writing standard English, the features that identify the standard must be there from the outset, or very soon after. And this means that specific items of vocabulary are next to useless. For what are the chances that the first few words in a discourse will contain *refute*, *disinterested*, or any of the others?

But the first few words of spoken discourse will definitely display one thing: pronunciation. No word can be spoken without a pronunciation. We shall discuss this in a later chapter. And in writing, the first few words will definitely display one thing: orthography. No word can be written without spelling, and no sentence without punctuation. We shall discuss this in a later chapter. And whether in speech or writing, the discourse will definitely display one major feature: grammar. No sentence can begin without grammar. And because grammar is common to both spoken and written language, it is of critical importance when it comes to defining a standard. We shall discuss this now.

Grammar is absolutely central to the study of language, in any of its dialects, standard or otherwise. It is so important because words by themselves do not make sense. A single word is usually ambiguous. What does this word mean?

charge

The problem is that it has too many meanings. It could be something to do with armies, or electricity, or costs, or several other things. But as soon as we put it into a sentence, then things begin to make sense.

> The cavalry made a charge down the hill.
> They are going to charge me for the drinks.
> The battery needs a charge.

That is what sentences do. That is what they are for. They exist in order to 'make' sense. Literally. They create it, by bringing words together into patterns. All the pieces and processes of sentence construction—clauses, phrases, nouns, articles, tenses...—are there to enable us to express and understand meanings. Some of these meanings are quite broad—such as who did what to whom (the 'subject— verb—object' construction); others are quite subtle, such as the distinction between *some* and *any* or between *which* and *that*. But the only reason we have such differences is to enable us to express contrasts of meaning. And grammar is the study of all the contrasts of meaning that it is possible to make within sentences. The 'rules' of grammar tell us how. By one count, there are some 3,500 such rules in English.

Young children learn about the importance of sentences around the age of eighteen months, when they put two words together and make a first stab at syntax. *See teddy*, says the child. *Teddy gone. Teddy there*. Before that, there were only individual words: *Teddy. Gone. There*. And, as every parent knows, that one-word stage is highly ambiguous. A sixteen-month-old approaches a parent and says *Push*. The parent waits to be pushed—but nothing happens. *Push*, says the child again, a little more forcefully. Ah, it is the child who wants to be pushed! A little later, that contrast will be clear from the arrangement of the words: *me push* vs. *push me*. The learning of syntax (a word which comes from the Greek, meaning 'arrangement') will have begun.

Grammar, I said above, is of critical importance when it comes to defining a standard. Not surprisingly, then, it became the focus of attention in the eighteenth century. And this is why Johnson's *Dictionary* did not suffice. Although his great work contained a sketch of English grammar at the front, and each word was assigned to its part of speech, it was not a serious attempt to present the grammar of the language. Nor had anyone else been able to fill the gap, since the early efforts of Bullokar and Jonson 150 years before (Chapter 9). Several attempts at an English grammar had been made, but none of them had become influential. Some were written in Latin. Others evidently lacked the required 'authority' (Chapter 13).

This was a major challenge to those who wanted to impose linguistic order on English. There had to be an authoritative grammar which would make it clear what the rules were. It would then be a straightforward matter to say, as soon as people spoke or wrote, whether they were using standard English or not. If they followed the rules, as prescribed by the grammar, they would be using standard English. If they didn't, they wouldn't be.

There is nothing wrong with the underlying logic of that paragraph. Linguistics scholars of all shapes and sizes agree that the grammar of a language has rules, that utterances which conform to those rules are 'grammatical' and those which don't are 'ungrammatical'. Linguists also recognize the distinction between 'standard' and 'non-standard' language. Many have written grammars of standard English—such as the huge *Comprehensive Grammar of the English Language* by Randolph Quirk and his associates, which appeared in 1985. So how did things go so horribly pear-shaped? Where did all the rows over grammar come from?

The quarrelling began because the eighteenth-century grammarians made two disastrous decisions. They forgot about diversity. And they got the rules wrong.

16

Appropriateness

GRAMMARIANS forgot about diversity? Perhaps 'forgot' is the wrong word. Apart from a tiny few, such as Johnson, there is little evidence that the social elite of the eighteenth century ever appreciated linguistic diversity in the first place.

'Polite' English—recall that the use of the term 'standard language' did not emerge until the end of the following century (Chapter 6)—was genteel and educated. Any failure to live up to its harsh criteria brought immediate social sanctions. *Punch*, a century later, would repeatedly satirize the unforgiving nature of the society which condemned people because of the way they spoke or wrote. A typical piece would show a group of people standing around a cowering wretch, looking down at him in horror. The caption: 'He split an infinitive.'

This is where linguists part company with eighteenth-century grammarians and their successors. Linguists do not question the importance of the standard dialect. It is an essential medium of communication in a diverse world. Indeed, it has always been their first object of study—not least, because it is so important in the study of literature and in teaching English as a foreign language. All the major grammars of English written by linguists have been grammars of the standard language.

But linguists do not dismiss all other dialects as inferior. Such dialects, in their view, are as expressive in their own way as anything to be found in the standard variety. They are simply different means of communication, designed for different purposes. Standard English emerged to solve a particular problem: the need for a national (and today an international) lingua franca. Regional dialects solve a different problem: the need to express local identities.

So, when an eighteenth-century grammarian (or a modern language pedant) says that *we was robbed* is 'bad English, and that's all there is to it', a student of modern linguistics would hotly disagree. It is simply non-standard English, perfectly 'good' in its own context. And there is indeed a lot more to it. As follows.

It would be inappropriate to use *we was robbed* in a serious piece of formal standard English. No argument there. A child who wrote this in an essay would deserve the red pencil. Equally, a child who said *we were robbed* to a group of his friends in the playground, bemoaning the fact that his side has just lost a football match because of a last-minute goal, would deserve his peers' equivalent of the red pencil. There the non-standard form is the appropriate one. That is the point that pedants forget.

Different usages are appropriate to different settings, and once we are aware of this we can begin to exploit the stylistic contrast involved. A newspaper sports editor wanting to write an eye-grabbing headline might switch from the customary standard English of the newspaper, and print: WE WUZ ROBBED. A novelist might represent the speech of a football supporter by putting 'We was robbed' in inverted commas. Competent writers know they have the ability to switch into and out of standard English, when there is an effect to be achieved. And this is one of the linguistic skills that children have to be taught.

It isn't just an occasional thing. Dozens of the best novels of the nineteenth century move effortlessly into and out of standard English. Think of Dickens, Emily Brontë, Walter Scott. And today, it is almost an unwritten law of novel-writing that there should be a liberal presence of non-standard English. Think of Irvine Welsh, Roddy Doyle, Suhayl Saadi. Nor is it only novels. Think poetry: Benjamin Zephaniah, John Agard. Think drama: virtually everyone.

Appropriateness in language is the same as appropriateness in other walks of life. Take clothing. If you looked into your wardrobe and found there only one suit of clothes, or one dress, how prepared would you feel to face the sartorial demands made upon you by society? No one would be happy if they had only the one option for all types of formal and informal occasion, for different days of the week, or for different functions, such as swimming, gardening, or washing a car. The more types of clothing we have, the better. But having a large and varied wardrobe is only useful if we have developed a 'clothes sense'.

We know what would happen if we disregarded a dress code on an invitation. We know how we feel if we wear the same clothes two days running—an issue which seems to affect Venus more than Mars, but in principle is applicable to everyone. We know how stupid it would be to use clothes that are totally inappropriate to the situation—or, of course, how daring. None of this is instinct. It is all social learning. And it starts at an early age. Parents let children know it if they dress inappropriately—whether by ignorance or intention. 'YOU CHANGE THOSE TROUSERS BEFORE YOU GO ON THAT BIKE!'

The application of this analogy is probably obvious, so just a few lines are needed to illustrate it. If children have only one variety of language to use, it is like having a single-item wardrobe. On the other hand, if they have been made aware of all the varieties in a language—by degrees, of course, during a language syllabus of several years—then they leave school linguistically fully dressed. And the more that adults who may have missed out on this kind of training take steps to familiarize themselves with the stylistic range of English, the more prepared they will be to interact effectively with people from all walks of life.

The fundamental principle of educational linguistics—to adapt the scouting slogan—is:

BE LINGUISTICALLY PREPARED.

And appropriateness is the key factor. One of the aims of education, whether by parents or by teachers, is to instil appropriate behaviour. If we behave inappropriately, we risk social sanctions. Language is a form of social behaviour, and it is subject to these sanctions as is everything else.

The main aim of language education has thus to be the instilling into children of a sense of linguistic appropriateness—when to use one variety or style rather than another, and when to appreciate the way in which other people have used one variety or style rather than another. This is what the eighteenth-century prescriptive approach patently did not do.

The prescriptive grammarians are so called precisely because they felt that people needed just a single variety of language for all occasions. 'Always do X and you will be fine.' 'Never do Y, and you will be fine.' The two types of rule, 'always' and 'never', are distinguished by different terms. Alongside *prescriptive*, we find *proscriptive*—a word which also arrived in English in the mid-eighteenth century. Prescriptive rules tell you what you should do. Proscriptive rules tell you what you shouldn't do.

As a means of surviving in high society, 'always' and 'never' may have their place. As a means of surviving in society as a whole, and especially in a modern multidimensional society, which makes a multiplicity of ethnic, specialist, and technological demands upon all of us, they are a disaster.

Nor do they help if our ambitions are more than mere survival. If you want to succeed, then it is even more important to have the ability to enter into rapport with people from all walks of life, regardless of the kind of English they speak or write. It is a matter of common experience that you will not do well if you criticize the English (or, for that matter, the foreign language) of someone you want to do business with, or fail to take into account their linguistic expectations. 'Do buy my goods—but by the way, I don't like your grammar.' 'Do buy my goods—but I'm going to tell you about them in a style you won't be able to understand.'

By contrast, the best recipe for success is to respect the varieties of language (or the other languages) that people use. The company that learns even a little bit of Japanese will do better in Japan than one which assumes that 'they all speak English'. We will all do better in a foreign country if we learn a bit of the language. And it is the same, in principle, within a language. We will all do better if we respect the way others have varied the language to form their own communities. And if we want to succeed in politics, business, religion, education, or any other walk of life, then acknowledging this is an essential early step. We shall see how twenty-first-century institutions have taken this message on board in a later chapter.

But this was not a palatable message in the eighteenth century. The error of the prescriptive grammarians is that they adopted a normative stance about usage. They assumed that one variety of language—the standard, as seen in formal written English—was the only variety worth using, the norm for everyone. They asserted that the rules of that variety were the only ones which could be called correct. Everything else was rubbish—informal writing, informal speaking, regional speaking or writing.

This approach to grammar—or to any other aspect of language—is not one we should espouse. That is the chief argument of this book. It is sad that it still has to be made, but the legacy of 200 years of prescriptive grammar-teaching in schools dies hard.

We must move on to some examples. But before doing so, an observation is in order. Anyone brought up on a diet of prescriptive grammar will surely be thinking that this whole argument is a quintessentially modern one, that it is a product of trendy liberal views. 'It's what you'd expect from Crystal, one of these permissive types,' said someone who had been wheeled out to debate a point of grammar with me on a radio programme once.

Modern it isn't. Almost as soon as the first grammarians made their first prescriptive rules, there were people pointing out that the whole approach was bunk. They said so a little more elegantly, of course. 'Our grammarians appear to me to have acted precipitately.' This isn't Crystal talking. It is Joseph Priestley, in an English grammar written 180 years before Crystal was born.

17

Incorrectness

JOSEPH Priestley's remark appeared in *The Rudiments of English Grammar*, published in 1761. He aligns himself with Ben Jonson, Quintilian, and others in affirming the importance of custom: 'It must be allowed, that the custom of speaking is the original and only just standard of any language.' This seems like such an obvious remark that we might wonder why he needed to make it. It was because he knew how the prescriptive grammarians were thinking.

Who were the prescriptive grammarians? And when did they write?

There is a remarkable period of twenty years in the mid-eighteenth century, from 1755 to 1775, which saw an explosion of influential prescriptive writing, affecting all areas of the language. Johnson's *Dictionary* marks the first date. John Walker's idea for an English pronouncing dictionary marks the second: 1774. The first major grammar falls within the middle of this period, in 1762. It was written by clergyman Robert Lowth, professor of poetry at Oxford, and Bishop of London at the height of his career.

Lowth's *Short Introduction to English Grammar* sets the tone, condemning the whole of English major literary output to date:

> The English language as it is spoken by the politest part of the nation, and as it stands in the writings of our most approved authors, oftentimes offends against every part of grammar.

No one was exempt, including all who had in previous generations themselves been critical of contemporary usage and put themselves forward as models of excellence. His book was less than 200 pages long, but he managed to criticize the language of Shakespeare, Milton, Dryden, Pope, Addison, Swift, and others, each of whom, in his opinion, had offended. They had all failed in their efforts to speak or write properly.

Lowth's book was widely read: it went into forty-five editions by 1800, and was the inspiration behind an even more widely used book, Lindley Murray's *English Grammar* of 1795. Murray was a New York lawyer and businessman who, in the 1780s, retired to England because of poor health. He settled in Holgate, in Yorkshire, where he was asked to provide some material on grammar for a local girls' school. His *Grammar*, which borrowed heavily from Lowth, was the result. The title in full:

> English Grammar, adapted to the different classes of learners; With an Appendix, containing Rules and Observations for Promoting Perspicuity in Speaking and Writing

It was the *Eats, Shoots and Leaves* of his day. It sold over 20 million copies, and was popular in the United States as well as in Britain. Twentieth-century school grammars—until the 1950s—would all trace their ancestry back to Murray.

When your name starts turning up in novels and plays, then you know you have made it. Charles Dickens, in Chapter 29 of *The Old Curiosity Shop* (1840–41), describes Mrs Jarley's efforts to attract a new class of audience to her waxworks:

> And these audiences were of a very superior description, including a great many young ladies' boarding-schools, whose favour Mrs Jarley had been at great pains to conciliate, by altering the face and costume of Mr Grimaldi as clown to represent Mr Lindley Murray as he appeared when engaged in the composition of his English Grammar.

We can see the prescriptive temperament at work if we follow through an individual example. A famous case is the rule that we should never end a sentence with a preposition (words like *to*, *from*, *of*). I remember being taught this in school. And I remember the English language examination I had to sit at the age of 16, in which I was presented with such questions as: 'Correct the following sentences.' They were sentences like this:

> That is the man I was talking to.

To get 100 per cent, I was expected to change this to:

> That is the man to whom I was talking.

And change it I did. I wanted to pass.

Only later did I begin to wonder why the first sentence was 'incorrect'. It is, after all, a type of sentence construction which is over a thousand years old in English. We find it in Old English texts. We find it in Chaucer. We find it in Shakespeare. Indeed, what is probably the most famous speech in the English language contains two instances of it. 'To be or not to be…'

> … The heartache and the thousand natural shocks
> That flesh is heir to.

> … And makes us rather bear those ills we have
> Than fly to others that we know not of.

So if putting a preposition at the end of a sentence has such an ancient and literary standing, why on earth was it eventually considered incorrect?

The short answer—and it applies to all prescriptive rules—is that somebody thought it was wrong. And that somebody managed to persuade everyone else to think in the same way. In an age when people were looking for reassurance and authority, anxious to find clear-cut ways for distinguishing 'us' from 'them', it is not surprising to find such prescriptions welcomed. For there is nothing quite as clear-cut as a grammatical distinction. Either a preposition goes at the end or it does not. There is no middle way. And the same applies to all the other famous prescriptions: either you split an infinitive or you don't; either you use two negatives or you don't. If you are wanting to make social distinctions, grammar is an easy way to do it.

In the case of the end-placed preposition, the somebody was John Dryden. As we saw in Chapter 10, Dryden was strongly critical of what he believed were errors in earlier writers. He picks on Ben Jonson, and finds this example:

> The Waves, and Dens of beasts cou'd not receive
> The bodies that those Souls were frighted from.

He comments:

> The Preposition in the end of the sentence; a common fault with him, and which I have but lately observ'd in my own writings.

Why did Dryden not like a preposition at the end of the sentence? It was probably a mixture of things. He may have developed a stylistic taste for finishing a sentence with an important word. He may have been impressed by the different rhythms involved in the alternatives. He may have sensed that the end-placing was very common in colloquial speech. But above all, Dryden, a classical scholar, would been influenced by Latin grammarians. In Latin, prepositions go before nouns. That is why they are called 'pre'-positions. As we saw in Chapter 1, there could be no higher accolade for a language than to imitate Latin.

Whatever the reason, Dryden took against the construction. And when he noticed that it was something he routinely did himself, he started correcting it in his own writing. Full marks for acting according to your principles, at any rate!

A century later, the prescriptive grammarians welcomed Dryden's decision with open arms. To see why, you have to appreciate what they were trying to do. Their aim was to find grammatical patterns which could characterize polite speech and writing. That meant formal English. The trouble is that there are not many possibilities in the language. If we add up all the features of grammar that distinguish formal from informal usage, we will not get a very large total—just a few dozen. And only a small number of these are at all common. Contracted forms of verbs (*I'm, they're*) are probably the most frequent indicators of informal speech or writing.

The prepositional issue was perfect. Not only had the rule been proposed by someone with immense literary prestige, but the kind of construction illustrated by *That is the man I was talking to* is very common in English, so the rule would act as a good discriminator. Eventually, it became one of the most widely known of all the prescriptive rules—perhaps only the proscription about splitting infinitives (*to boldly go*) would become more famous.

It achieved the peak of its fame when a criticism of the rule was attributed to Winston Churchill in the 1940s. The story was circulating that an over-zealous editor had corrected one of Churchill's end-placed prepositions, and he is supposed to have written in the margin: 'This is the sort of bloody nonsense up with which I will not put.' The story may be apocryphal, and the exact phrasing of the remark varies with the teller. It is also a bit of a cheat, as the effect is achieved only by fracturing an idiom (to *put up with* something), and this use of *with* would in any case be called an adverb, in traditional grammar, and not a preposition at all! But it has nonetheless become a catch-phrase, and might easily have been the title of this book.

Notice that this kind of example increases the range of constructions thought to be improper in English. Regional dialect grammar, as we have seen, was one source of 'incorrectness'. But there is nothing especially regional about putting a preposition at the end of a sentence. All dialects do it—including standard English. It is a core feature of English grammar, and always has been. But it is avowedly informal. And evidently prescriptive grammarians felt that colloquial constructions were not 'polite' either.

Some prescriptivists acknowledged the difficulty. Murray himself did. In discussing the topic he actually says:

> This is an idiom to which our language is strongly inclined;
> it prevails in common conversation, and suits very well with
> the familiar style in writing.

If he had left the matter there, all might indeed have been well. But there is a but:

> but the placing of the preposition before the relative [i.e. the
> pronouns *which* and *whom*, in the examples above and on
> page 109] is more graceful, as well as more perspicuous...

More graceful? That is a matter of taste. And more perspicuous? Murray is saying that putting the preposition in the middle makes the meaning clearer. That is absolute nonsense. There are certainly several grammatical rules where we could argue that one alternative is clearer or easier to understand than the other (the distinction between active and passive voice, for instance), but this rule is not one of them.

The two prepositional constructions are undoubtedly different, from a stylistic point of view. *That is the man to whom I was talking* is much more formal than *That is the man I was talking to*. The former usage would be appropriate if we were writing a scientific report, for example: *There are at least twenty-five species to which the name 'daffodil' has been given*. Most science editors would prefer this to the alternative: *There are at least twenty-five species which the name 'daffodil' has been given to*. We have to say 'most' because tastes do vary, and there are always cases where either alternative would be acceptable. But for every instance of an end-placed preposition in science texts there will be a hundred middle-placed examples. And the reverse frequency obtains in informal settings, where we far less likely to hear or see *That is the man to whom I was talking*.

Modern school language examinations reflect this change of emphasis. The question is no longer phrased in terms of 'correct' vs. 'incorrect'. Rather, students might be given the alternatives and asked to discuss when one version would be used and when the other. Or they might be given a text and asked to discuss the features which make it formal or informal. In a novel, where we will find both constructions reflecting different kinds of character and situation, the question might be: explain the variation. In all cases, the examiner wants to find out if students are aware of the stylistic difference. It is a much more interesting question than the one I was asked all those years ago. It is also much harder to get 100 per cent. But it is a better linguistic education.

What would prescriptive grammarians have said, if we were able to point out to them that Shakespeare, for example, frequently put prepositions at the end of sentences? We know the answer, because they noticed this themselves, and they remark upon it. What they say, in effect, is this: 'There you are, you see. Even Shakespeare gets it wrong. And if one of our best writers can make such a stupid mistake, what chance have you, O reader, of doing better? But do not worry. Help is at hand, in the form of this grammar. Read and obey, and all shall be well.'

Not everyone agreed that all was well. A number of critics tried to introduce a sense of reality into the situation, but they were ignored. And for the next 250 years, people were lulled into a false sense of linguistic security by the assurances of the prescriptive grammarians. But, as we shall see, you can't fool all of the people all of the time.

18

Perspicuity

I N what way were the prescriptive grammarians fooling us? The clue lies in the *p*-words that writers such as Lowth and Murray sprinkled throughout their work. We have already noted 'politeness'. 'Promoting perspicuity' appears in Murray's title; and the opening sentence of his book reads:

> English Grammar is the art of speaking and writing the English language with propriety.

The three chapters forming the first part of his appendix are headed: 'Of purity', 'Of propriety', and 'Of precision'. What did Murray mean by 'perspicuity'. It is, he says,

> the fundamental quality of style: a quality so essential in every kind of writing that for the want of it nothing can atone... it is a degree of positive beauty.

These are fine words; but what exactly is the basis of this quality? As already suggested in Chapter 17, it seems to be clarity:

> We are pleased with an author, and consider him as deserving praise, who frees us from all fatigue of searching for his meaning.

No one could possibly disagree with that sentiment.

But we have already seen the difficulty earlier writers faced when they tried to impose rules on the notion of clarity. Recall the fate of Thomas Sprat, in Chapter 10. Murray falls into the same trap. He thinks that if he bans certain kinds of usage, clarity will be the result. If only it were so easy.

His appendix, as mentioned above, insists on three qualities of style. 'Purity' is the first. It is a familiar theme:

> The introduction of foreign and learned words, unless where necessity requires them, should never be admitted into our composition. Barren languages may need such assistance, but ours is not one of these.

Rather, people should work towards 'a plain, native style'. It is Sprat reborn. And, as with all earlier (and later) writers who take up this position, he is fooling himself, and trying to fool us. The paragraph in which he makes these remarks is 107 words long; 33 of them—virtually all the meaty words— are from Latin or French. Even the phrase 'plain, native style' is totally French in origin.

He then turns to 'Propriety', which is defined in a way that hardly lives up to his own demand for perspicuity:

> Propriety of language is the selection of such words as the best usage has appropriated to those ideas which we intend to express by them; in opposition to low expressions, and to words and phrases which would be less significant of the ideas that we mean to convey.

He then gives a list of criteria for achieving this goal. Some of them, such as his recommendation to avoid ambiguous words, or his advice not to use a word too frequently, are fine. Others display only his personal taste. 'We must avoid low expressions,' he says, and illustrates by *topsy turvy*, *hurly burly*, *pellmell*, and such idioms as *currying favour* and *dancing attendance*. He ends his selection with '&c'. It is of course impossible to continue such a list in a consistent way. Not even other authors of the age agreed with him. Johnson, for example, has entries on *topsy turvy*, *hurly burly*, and *pellmell*. None of them are called low.

Probably the most absurd of his recommendations under this heading is the avoidance of 'an exuberance of metaphor'. It is absurd because it leads him to exclude most of the genre of poetry. John Dryden's lines are singled out:

> From harmony, from heavenly harmony,
> This universal frame began...

and said to show 'scarcely a glimpse of meaning'. Try harder, Dryden.

Murray's third quality of style is 'Precision'. He defines it—in an exuberance of metaphor—as follows:

It signifies retrenching superfluities, and pruning the expression so as to exhibit neither more nor less than an exact copy of the person's idea who uses it.

All he means, judging by his examples, is that in formal usage we should pay careful attention to the nuances of meaning which differentiate synonyms, such as the distinction between *pride* and *vanity* or *entire* and *complete*. No one would disagree with that.

That last paragraph illustrates the paradox about prescriptive grammarians, as well as about present-day usage pundits. They all talk sense some of the time. Of course clarity is important. Of course it is important to distinguish meanings where there are meanings to be distinguished. Of course it is good to aim for an effective and elegant style, however those qualities are defined.

But they spoil everything by talking nonsense the rest of the time. It is just plain daft to try to reduce such complex notions as clarity and elegance to a few basic rules. It is even dafter to invent some rules—or borrow them from Latin—to make your point. When people do that, they display the artificiality of the situation very quickly by breaking the rules themselves, in their own writing.

This, of course, provides critics with excellent ammunition. Every usage book, old or new, contains such lines as these:

I am not one of these stupid pundits who thinks that X is a problem.
However, I can't stand Y.

For X, read 'split infinitive', 'preposition ending', 'the distinction between *will* and *shall*', or whatever takes your fancy. For Y, read the same list. All a reviewer has to do is look through the book finding examples of what the writer has banned. The typical review of a usage book has such lines as these:

So-and-so condemns usage X.
However, he (or she) uses X on page 76.

The more an author attempts to simplify a complex aspect of language, the more these comments are easy to make—and other pundits are always ready to make them. It is a cut-throat world, usage. Most critical reviews of *Eats, Shoots and Leaves* contained caustic remarks about the way Lynne Truss's own use of commas, for example, left a great deal to be desired (Chapter 20).

Murray was no exception. For example, in talking about perspicuity in grammar, he homes in on the Dryden rule about prepositions and generalizes it. To maintain the 'strength' of sentences, he says, we must 'avoid concluding them with an adverb, a preposition, or any inconsiderable word'—by which he means (from the examples he gives) pronouns such as *it*. He gives as a 'disagreeable' instance, a sentence ending with *in it*. Yet, turn over the page and we find a sentence ending in *it* and two ending in *them*.

An unrealistic rule is bound to be broken, because it is not a part of the language—only a part of the rule inventor's imaginings. Once the inventor's attention is distracted, the natural usage is bound to reassert itself. Indeed, because rule inventors do not look carefully at the language as a whole, they fail to notice instances where they have no choice in the matter—where their rule simply will not work. In this next example, Murray has no choice: it is impossible to put the final particle into the middle of the sentence:

> When they [the elements of a sentence] have a regular and proportional division, they are much easier to the voice, are more clearly understood, and better remembered, than when this rule is not attended to.

If this were an isolated case, we might not worry. But there are several more like it, and some are even more puzzling. Take the supposed distinction between *will* and *shall*. This goes back to a Latin grammar of English published by the mathematician John Wallis in 1653. Murray insists on the same sharp distinction:

> *Will*, in the first person singular and plural, intimates resolution and promising: in the second and third person, only foretells. ... *Shall*, on the contrary, in the first person, simply foretells; in the second and third persons, promises, commands, or threatens.

It all sounds very neat and logical, so he uses it to condemn, for example, Psalm 23 from the King James Bible:

> The following passage is not translated according to the distinct and proper meanings of the words *shall* and *will*: 'Surely goodness and mercy shall follow me all the days of my life; and I will dwell in the house of the Lord for ever;' it ought to be, '*Will* follow me;' and 'I *shall* dwell.'

Some uses of *shall* in English (then and now) *are* different from *will*. If drowning, I would strongly recommend you not to shout *No one shall save me*. But the vast majority of statements where we want to express future time are not like this. Most people use the forms indiscriminately, and have done so for centuries: *I will/shall get some stamps at the post office.*

There is a famous recorded instance. A few years ago, the *Daily Star* ran a front-page headline reporting the words of a member of the royal family who had done something newsworthy: it read I SHALL HAVE TO LIVE WITH IT. On the same day, *The Sun* reported the same story with the same size of headlines: I WILL HAVE TO LIVE WITH IT.

The prescriptive grammarians went out of their way to invent as many rules as possible which might distinguish polite from impolite speech. They didn't find very many—just a few dozen, a tiny number compared with all the thousands of rules of grammar that operate in English (Chapter 15). But these rules were propounded with maximum authority and severity, and given plausibility by the claim that they were going to help people to be clear and precise. As a result, generations of schoolchildren would be taught them, and be confused by them.

I remember my own schooldays' confusion over such matters as *will* and *shall*. The marks on my hands have now faded. I suffered—unnecessarily—because I failed to appreciate a non-existent distinction imposed upon me by a school teacher conned by the legacy of Lindley Murray. I was one of millions.

And when I see people still being conned—made to feel threatened or inferior because a linguistically brainwashed boss or radio listener or teacher threatens all hell if infinitives are split or prepositions ended, then I get cross. And when I see the same rubbish being promulgated 250 years on—still, in this day and age—in books written by well-intentioned people who say they care about the language while cheerfully admitting to not having any qualifications at all to talk about it, then I get very cross. And when I see their books being bought by millions, I am amazed at the way the con still has such power to succeed. That is why the very first article I ever wrote, in the *Liverpool Echo* way back in 1962, was an attack on prescriptive grammar. And why, forty-four years later, I am still at it.

If I were alone in this fight, I might well conclude that it is me who is paranoid. But I am just the latest in a long line of critics who have tried to stop the rot. Joseph Priestley, as we saw in Chapter 16, was one of the first. Thomas de Quincey, writing in 1839, was another. He listed a series of grammars from Ben Jonson's on, and concluded:

> We have also, and we mention it on account of its great but most unmerited popularity, the grammar of Lindley Murray.... This book, full of atrocious blunders... reigns despotically through the young ladies' schools, from the Orkneys to the Cornish Scillys.

And as late as 1869, we find in an issue of *The Athanaeum* an article headed 'The Bad English of Lindley Murray and other Writers on the English Language'.

All these critics failed to stop the growth in the prescriptive temperament. The time was not right. Things would begin to change only towards the end of the twentieth century.

19

Clarity

I T is such a shame. There is a lot of good stuff in the prescriptive grammars. They were written by people with considerable experience of using English, and they are full of good ideas which we can all learn from. Murray's book contains many accurate observations about English grammar. I have written a grammar myself, and you would be hard pressed to see the difference, a lot of the time.

It is the same with the modern manifestations of usage paranoia. The books contain much that is linguistically illuminating and uncontentious. They often draw attention to genuine points of ambiguity, and they can warn people about areas of usage where it is easy to be unclear. Excellent. Then the authors spoil it by homing in on aspects of usage which fail to recognize the shifting complexity of the linguistic world, and which are nothing to do with clarity at all. They propose solutions to language problems which cannot possibly work. And they charge you for it. Sometimes quite a lot, as you will know if you have ever replied to one of those advertisements promising to solve all your usage difficulties in one go.

They ought to be had up under the Trades Descriptions Act. Or run out of town, like the nineteenth-century quacks who claimed that their patent medicines would cure all ills. It is all (as Paul Newman's character in *The Sting* put it) a 'big con'.

The big con is to be told that the rules, if you follow them, will help you to be clear. But that is what most of the rules do not do. As we have seen in the previous chapters, there is no difference in clarity if you put a preposition in the middle or at the end of a sentence. The meanings are the same. Nor is there a difference in meaning between most uses of *will* and *shall*. Nor, to move on, is there usually any difference in meaning if you split an infinitive or not.

This was a rule which escaped Murray's attention. It didn't appear in grammar books until the nineteenth century. It was another example of Latin reasoning. The infinitive form of a verb is one which gives you just the basic form, without adding any endings to express such meanings as tense, person, and number. The verb is in its naked state, ready to take on any meaning you throw at it. It is not delimited in any way. As the Latin grammarians said, 'It has no finitude.' Hence the name: 'infinitive'.

In English the infinitive is typically presented as two words: *to love, to go*. In Latin, an inflected language, there is just one: *ire, amare*. If you want to add an adverb, to express such meanings as how or when or where you are loving, then you don't have the option to insert it within the verb—to say, in effect, *am-ADVERB-are*. But you do in English.

In English, we can say *to boldly love*, and it is this separation of the *to* from the verb which is called the 'split infinitive'. It is a construction which has been in the language for centuries. It is popular because it is rhythmically more natural to say. The basic rhythm of English is a 'tum-te-tum' rhythm—what in the main tradition of English poetry is called an *iambic pentameter*, with strong (*stressed*) and weak (*unstressed*) syllables alternating:

The <u>cur</u>few <u>tolls</u> the <u>knell</u> of <u>part</u>ing <u>day</u>...

The strong syllables are underlined. When we split an infinitive we are striving to achieve this rhythm. Let us see why.

The *to* part of an infinitive carries no stress. And adverbs in English usually end in *-ly*, which also carries no stress. So of the three options, only one follows the basic heart-beat of English:

<u>bold</u>ly to <u>love</u>   strong—weak—weak—strong
to <u>love</u> <u>bold</u>ly   weak—strong—strong—weak
to <u>bold</u>ly <u>love</u>   weak—strong—weak—strong

That is why we do it. If you want to use one of the other possibilities, you can. It is a matter of stylistic taste, and that's all it is. But the split version is the more native.

So, don't be fooled when a grammarian tells you, 'Ah, but one is clearer than the other.' It isn't. The three forms above convey exactly the same meaning. If you let yourself believe otherwise, you have been taken in by the big con.

The split version is the norm. Things start to get linguistically interesting when we look for the exceptions.

Clarity

There are usually exceptions to grammatical rules, prescriptive or otherwise. That is one of the reasons why grammar is such a fascinating subject of study. So, be prepared for the occasional example where changing the position of the adverb *does* change the meaning of the sentence. Examples like this:

They failed completely to understand the problem.
They failed to completely understand the problem.

There are not many examples like this, but they do present real issues of clarity. Unfortunately, the prescriptive grammarians don't discuss them.

That is the other side of the con. We all need to learn how to be clear. But the prescriptive grammars don't tell us about the most important ways to achieve this goal. And their obsession with detail can distract us from the broader picture.

Only is a good example. Some books spend pages worrying about where *only* should go in a sentence. Some of the worry is unnecessary. There is no problem when the context makes it absolutely clear what is meant, as in:

I only bought two tickets, and I should have bought three.

But there can be a problem when the context is unclear, as in:

I only advised Mary.

The meaning is usually clear in speech, where the way we stress the words will distinguish the two meanings:

I <u>only</u> <u>advised</u> Mary—I didn't tell her.
I <u>only</u> advised <u>Mary</u>—not John.

But you can't see this in writing, so there is indeed a possibility of ambiguity. In these circumstances, it would be wise be aware of the danger, and to place *only* next to the word it modifies—*I advised only Mary*—or, of course, to rephrase the sentence.

Some people worry endlessly about where *only* should go. They spend ages locating their *only*s perfectly—and yet their language can still be unclear. That is because *only* is only a drop in the ocean of clarity. There are more things in heaven and earth entering into the notion of clarity than are dreamed of in prescriptivist philosophy. And the grammar pundits never mention them.

This isn't a grammar book, so I mustn't go on for too long; but let me take just one example of an important clarity principle. Which of the following two sentences do you find clearer?

> It was nice having John and Mary come and see us the other day.
> Having John and Mary come and see us the other day was nice.

I have put this choice before thousands of people, over the years, and they always opt for the first. Why?

It is all to do with the length of the subject—that part of the sentence which precedes the verb in a statement. Here are the sentences again, with the subjects underlined:

> <u>It</u> was nice having John and Mary come and see us the other day.
> <u>Having John and Mary come and see us the other day</u> was nice.

We do not like long subjects. Three-quarters of the subjects that we use in everyday speech consist of just one word (<u>*She*</u> *is in the garden,* <u>*I*</u> *went down the street*) or a short noun phrase (<u>*The woman*</u> *was in the garden,* <u>*The children*</u> *went down the street*). The longer the subject gets, the more uncomfortable we feel. If you don't believe me, try this next example, and note the point where you start to scream.

> The real importance of this issue, critical to any discussion of the matter, and directly related to the other issues already discussed in this book, in the various chapters which deal with points about perspicuity, a topic of undoubted significance to all of us, and a topic moreover which will continue to be of importance...

It is an absurdly long subject. You need the main verb in order to know what to 'do' with this subject. And I am not giving you one.

The longer a writer (or speaker) makes you wait for a main verb, the more you have to 'process' the subject, holding it in your short-term memory. It is much easier to process a sentence if the main verb comes relatively early on. Notice how much more comfortable the silly example becomes if I begin with a verb:

> I will now discuss the real importance of this issue, critical to any discussion of the matter, and directly related to the other issues already discussed in this book, in the various chapters which deal with points about perspicuity, a topic of undoubted significance to all of us, and a topic moreover which will continue to be of importance...

It is still a silly sentence, but at least you feel you are more in control of it now. That verb *discuss* helps enormously.

The basic grammatical principle is this: it is clearer, in English, to keep the weight away from the subject and locate it after the verb. You can depart from this principle if you like, but beware if you do.

Once we know this principle, we can apply it in all kinds of ways. For instance, when children are learning to read, it makes sense to keep the subjects of their sentences quite short. They will find it much easier to read this:

Jane saw the three little pigs with their mother.

than to read this:

The three little pigs with their mother saw Jane.

In fact, reading books often fall foul of this principle, and present the child with unnecessary difficulty as a result. The following are extracts from two versions of a well-known fairy tale. This one breaks the long-subject principle:

Turkey Lurkey, Ducky Lucky, Cocky Locky, Henny Penny, and Chicken Licken all walked into Foxy Loxy's den.

And this one doesn't.

Foxy Loxy ate up Turkey Lurkey, Ducky Lucky, Cocky Locky, Henny Penny, and Chicken Licken.

Not that it mattered much, either way, to Chicken Licken. There are more important things in life, and death, than grammar.

20

Punctuation

MORE important things than grammar? Yes, according to some—punctuation. Apostrophes, in particular. I don't know of any Society for the Protection of Infinitives. But I do know a Society for the Protection of the Apostrophe.

Readers who paid attention to my Preface, with its head-scratching over punctuation, will perhaps be surprised to find the topic only being dealt with now, in Chapter 20. But there is a reason. In the evolution of standard English, punctuation was the last feature people paid attention to. Spelling, vocabulary, and grammar had all been given a workover. Not punctuation. The topic is given just a few pages in Murray's *Grammar*, buried at the back of the book, and that is where it tends to stay, even in modern works.

It is a pity, because punctuation is much more than a grammatical afterthought. That is why I got so excited when I worked with Lynne Truss. As I said in the Preface, if anyone could make the subject sexy, she could. And she did. Her book is humorous, clever, clear, pretty accurate, well crafted, and deeply unnerving.

Zero tolerance. She uses metaphors of vigilantes, bala-clavas, militant wing, criminal damage. It's a joke, of course. Yes, it has to be a joke. But it's a funny sort of joke. She kindly refers to me in her preface as one among several who have been 'inspirational'. I hope I didn't inspire that.

In fact, I know I didn't. She makes it clear at one point that it was the secretary of the Apostrophe Protection Society who triggered 'the awakening of my Inner Stickler'. But even he must have been taken aback by the sudden militancy of her reaction. Society members, she says, write courteous letters to those shopkeepers who misuse apostrophes. She wants to go in with all linguistic guns blazing.

I agree totally with her underlying message, which is to bring the study of punctuation back into the centre of the educational stage. I am as disturbed as she is when I see the rules of standard English punctuation broken. As I have emphasized in earlier chapters, the whole point of a standard language is to ensure general intelligibility and acceptability by having everyone follow an agreed set of norms of usage. One of the jobs of education is to teach the written standard, and punctuation is part of that. If kids leave school not having learned to punctuate, then something has gone horribly wrong.

In a later chapter I'll talk about when things went wrong, and what is now being done to put things right. Here, I just want to point out why a 'zero tolerance' approach to punctuation, or to any aspect of English usage, is so misconceived.

Zero tolerance does not allow for flexibility. It is prescriptivism taken to extremes. It suggests that the language is in a state where all the rules are established with 100 per cent certainty. The suggestion is false. We do not know what all the rules of punctuation are. And no rule of punctuation is followed by all of the people all of the time.

Punctuation has always been a matter of trends. Commas, hyphens, semicolons, apostrophes—all have been subject to changes in fashion. In the seventeenth century the trend was to capitalize all nouns; in the eighteenth century, the trend was to leave the capitals out. Lindley Murray gave them the kiss of death, calling noun capitalization a 'troublesome' practice.

No one has ever been able to define a set of rules which will explain all uses of all punctuation marks. The selection of uses Lynne describes in *Eats, Shoots and Leaves* is only part of the story. Practice varies so much between formal and informal writing, between Britain and America, between page and screen, between publisher and publisher, between author and author, between generation and generation. The best we can do is identify and teach trends, and be very cautious indeed about making generalizations.

If you are not cautious, then be prepared to be taken to task. The 'dog eats dog' mentality of prescriptive critics gave Lynne a mauling, when her book first appeared. A reviewer in the *New Yorker* pointed out one punctuation error after another, beginning with her opening page:

The first punctuation mistake... appears in the dedication, where a nonrestrictive clause is not preceded by a comma.

And he goes on to note inconsistencies in her practice throughout the book.

This is one kind of zero tolerance being eaten by another. And yet both sides know very well that the matter is not so cut and dried. Lynne says herself at one point, talking about a use of the apostrophe, 'there are no absolute rights and wrongs in this matter'. She knows that punctuation is partly an art: she devotes a whole chapter to this topic. She knows about fashions and language change and all of that. So why didn't she adopt a more sympathetic attitude towards people who have problems?

Let's take one of her main apostrophe hates: the mixing up of *it's* and *its*. Here the situation is indeed clear-cut. The nineteenth-century printers and grammarians worked out the rules, and told everyone to follow them. It was all going to be so simple. Use the apostrophe either to show possession or to show an omitted letter. So: *cat*, *cat's*, and *cats'* for the former; *I've* and *there's* for the latter.

Generations of children had the first rule drummed into them. The apostrophe marks possession. The apostrophe marks possession. The apostrophe marks possession. And they started to write *cat's*, *dog's*, and *horse's*, just as they were supposed to do. Then they encountered *its*.

Its expresses possession. Compare:

The cat's food is in the bowl.
Its food is in the bowl.

And there you have the anomaly. *Its* is just as possessive as *cat's*, but it doesn't have an apostrophe. Why not?

Because the printers and grammarians never thought the matter through. They applied their rule to nouns and forgot about pronouns, thus creating an exception (along with *the food is hers, ours, yours, theirs*) without realizing it. And even if they had noticed, they wouldn't have done anything about it, for *it's* was already 'taken', as it were, as the abbreviation of *it is*.

But now look at it from the child's point of view. Teacher has told me that there is a definite correlation between the meaning of possession and the apostrophe. *Its food* has the meaning of possession. Therefore I will insert an apostrophe and I will get praise. *It's food*. And what does the poor child get instead? Blistering hellfire.

I really would have expected Lynne to be more sympathetic. After all, she went through just such a period of confusion herself. She tells us about one of her stratagems in her introduction. She would, she says,

> cunningly suspend a very small one immediately above the 's', to cover all eventualities. Imagine my teenage wrath when, time after time, my homework returned with this well-meant floating apostrophe struck out. 'Why?' I would rail, using all my powers of schoolgirl inference and getting nowhere.

Many children have grown up confused by *it's* and *its*, and they remain so as adults. It doesn't have to be that way. Good teaching can point out the exception and explain it. I always tell my students about the way the printers thought—or failed to think—and it helps enormously. Lynne didn't get that perspective. Indeed, she got nothing at all.

She went to grammar school, she tells us, in the late 1960s, when formal work on language was out. I was luckier. I went in the mid-1950s, when it was definitely in. I never had a problem with *it's* and *its*.

I don't feel I want to kill, even in jest, when I meet someone who still mixes up *it's* and *its*. I don't call them lazy, or careless, or harangue them with shouts of 'you should know better'. Something deeper is wrong here. They have evidently not been taught properly about how their language works. So whose fault was that?

I would make the same kind of argument about the other major apostrophe hate: the use of an apostrophe in such words as *potato's*. Lynne knows exactly why it's there. We talked a lot about it during her radio recording, and the reasons are given in her book. It's because *potato* is a word ending in a vowel—an unusual ending for an English word. Simply adding an *-s* would promote the misleading pronunciation 'pot-at-oss'. If you are unsure about the spelling (*potatoes*), then you will try to solve the problem using punctuation. Inserting an apostrophe is as good a way as any of showing there is an unusual plural. After all, we have done the same thing elsewhere for other unusual words, such as *1960's* and *JP's*.

Once again, if you have had a good language-based education, you will not find this a problem. But if you have not, then I am not surprised that you remain confused. And my instinct is to help, to explain—in a word, to teach. Not to threaten death and destruction.

For one brief moment, I thought that Lynne had taken this point. In discussing the issue she says:

> The only illiteracy with apostrophes that stirs any sympathy in me is the greengrocer's variety. First, because greengrocers are self-evidently horny-thumbed people who do not live by words. And second, because I agree with them that something rather troubling and unsatisfactory happens to words ending in vowels…

It's humorous, once again, but lurking beneath the surface there's an eighteenth-century 'us vs. them' attitude here which I find unpalatable. I know some greengrocers who are avid readers. And there's a curious double-think going on. 'I agree with them,' she says. With whom? With the green-grocers? On the one hand, she says greengrocers don't live by words; on the other, they are evidently so linguistically aware that they know about the problems of words ending in vowels.

Maybe it's just a slip in the writing. Maybe it's just an odd sense of humour. Having read the book several times now, I still am no nearer knowing whether the newspaper commentators I mentioned in my Preface—who think the book is a 'hoax' and a 'joke'—have a point. She writes about the topic with great good humour. She has the best of intentions. Her heart seems to be in the right place. So I would have expected tolerance of other people's educational handicaps, rather than the opposite. It's a puzzle.

21

Antecedents

L ET me begin by making a very important point…
No, let me rewrite that.

Let me begin by making a very important point it is perfectly possible to write a whole paragraph without any punctuation at all and everything still makes sense it may be a bit difficult to read in places because we are not used to seeing english written in this way also the technique makes us read in a rush but there is no real problem only every now and again would the lack of a punctuation mark make us stop and wonder what the writer meant

I could go on like this for pages. James Joyce does precisely that, in Molly Bloom's soliloquy at the end of *Ulysses*. And several other authors have experimented with the effect of leaving out aspects of punctuation. George Bernard Shaw was one. An indefatigable advocate of spelling reform, he avoided apostrophes whenever he could, and robustly defended his practice:

> The apostrophes in ain't, don't, haven't, etc. look so ugly that the most careful printing cannot make a page of colloquial dialogue as handsome as a page of classical dialogue. Besides,

shan't should be sha'n't, if the wretched pedantry of indicating the elision is to be carried out. I have written aint, dont, havnt [*sic*], shant, shouldnt, and wont for twenty years with perfect impunity, using the apostrophe only where its omission would suggest another word: for example, hell for he'll. There is not the faintest reason for persisting in the ugly and silly trick of peppering pages with these uncouth bacilli. I also write thats, whats, lets, for the colloquial forms of that is, what is, let us; and I have not yet been prosecuted.

You might think it unusual to have no punctuation at all, but that is in fact how English was written at the very beginning. Early manuscripts had no punctuation. They often didn't even have spaces between words. The earliest conventions were introduced as a guide to phrasing when reading aloud became an important activity, such as when it was necessary to read a text aloud in a religious service.

There was a great deal of experiment. Over thirty marks can be found in medieval manuscripts—various combinations of dots, curls, and dashes. Most of them disappeared after the arrival of printing. Some of them look like modern marks, but their function was not the same: a point, for example, represented a pause, rather than a sentence ending, and the height of the point could vary to express degrees of pause.

Printers had to make decisions about punctuation and capitalization as well as about spelling. The earliest European printers generally followed the marks they found in the manuscripts, the actual shapes depending on the typeface used. Most recognized three kinds of pause, represented by a point, a virgule (/), and a mark of interrogation. Caxton chiefly used a virgule and point (.), occasionally a colon (:) and paragraph mark (¶). Word-breaks at the end of a line were shown by a double virgule (//). The comma began to replace the virgule in the 1520s, though some printers used them interchangeably for a while.

Towards the end of the fifteenth century, semicircular parentheses, the question mark, and the semicolon, as well as the comma, were introduced in Europe, but it took some time for them all to appear in England. A single semicolon (until the mid-seventeenth century called by various names, such as *comma-colon* and *hemi-colon*) turns up in Paris in 1538. English printers did not begin using it until the 1570s.

Compositors found most of the new marks confusing, and there is a great deal of inconsistency of usage, especially when several people worked on the same book. Some marks were virtually interchangeable—and even in modern editions a comparison of two editions (e.g. of Shakespeare's *Sonnets*) will bring to light a remarkable range of decisions about which sets of lines should be separated by a colon, semi-colon, comma, or point.

Uncertainty always surrounds a new punctuation mark. In the sixteenth century there was great confusion among compositors over the use of the apostrophe. At first they used it only as a marker of an omitted letter; its use as a marker of possession came much later, in the eighteenth century. The hyphen, used to identify a compound word, and the exclamation mark (the 'note of admiration', as it was often called) arrived towards the end of the sixteenth century. It took a long time for the use of these marks to achieve some sort of stability.

In fact, of course, they never did totally stabilize. To take just one variable, the use of the hyphen: there are hundreds of variations in English. Do we write *flower-pot*, *flowerpot*, or *flower pot*? Is it *washing-machine* or *washing machine*? *cooperate* or *co-operate*? Publishers compile long lists in their style sheets to ensure consistency. No two publishers have the same list. I know, because I have published with many firms, over the years, and my hyphenated forms see-saw wildly from book to book. When I edit my own encyclopedias, my editorial team works with our own hyphenation list. It's different from everyone else's. With punctuation, the standard language is not as standard as we might think. It is the same with spelling, as we shall see in the next chapter.

The prescriptive grammarians desperately tried to find rules to control the messy situation. Lindley Murray opted for a phonetic solution based on a mathematical principle:

> The Comma represents the shortest pause; the Semicolon, a pause double that of the comma; the Colon, double that of the semicolon; and the Period, double that of the colon.

Imagine trying to put these principles to work in practice.

Practice defied such simplifications. 'Heavy punctuators' would spray commas all over their text; 'light punctuators' would avoid them. Even today, there is a choice between publishing house-styles over some uses of the comma.

Take the 'serial comma', which is present in the first phrase but absent in the second:

the tall, dark, and handsome auctioneer...
the tall, dark and handsome auctioneer...

Whichever one you prefer, it is plain that the two phrases could be read at exactly the same speed and without any difference in the way the reader pauses.

There are areas of uncertain usage in punctuation, along-side those areas where the rules are clear (as in the example of *it's* and *its*). We have to learn to manage both. It's a complex situation, and nothing is to be gained by oversimplifying it, or insisting that one person's personal taste in commas should be the yardstick for everyone. The history of punctuation shows that the complexity does not disappear. Rather, it changes as time goes by. And it is continuing to change. The biggest changes in punctuation since the Renaissance are about to hit us, because of the Internet. In a later chapter I'll discuss ways in which we can learn to manage them. We have to manage them. I don't know what the alternative is. Blow up the Internet, I suppose, if we continue with a policy of zero tolerance.

In the 1990s I thought we were entering an era where a more flexible attitude to language was becoming routine. I could sense it in the way the new National Curriculum was reintroducing formal language study into schools, but with an emphasis on explanation rather than prescription. Grammar was back, but now kids were being asked to explain grammatical variations, not to blindly condemn them.

For the first time in English linguistic history, there was hope of a rapprochement between the study of the standard language, which is so important for promoting universal intelligibility, and the study of non-standard language, which is so important for promoting local identity. *Eats, Shoots and Leaves* has been a huge setback to the installing of those positive values. I hope it's a one-off.

Despite its huge sales, it might well be. I asked twenty people whether they had a copy of *Eats, Shoots and Leaves*. Fifteen had. Five had bought it for themselves; ten had been given it as a present. One had been given two copies. Seven said they had read the whole thing. The rest 'were reading' it. I know what that means. I 'am reading' Stephen Hawkins's *A Brief History of Time*. It has been on my bookshelf for years. I marked the place where it got tricky, and I stopped. I will get back to it one day. I will, honestly. And then I will know all about time.

The ones who hadn't finished it said just that. They were intending to get back to it. Quite soon, in fact. Then they would know all about punctuation.

I asked the ones who had finished it what they thought. They had all enjoyed it. They found it an entertaining read. I asked them whether they thought it had done them any good, punctuationally speaking. It had indeed made them more aware of the issues. What issues? The errors that people make. But had it changed their own punctuational practice? They shifted uncomfortably on their feet.

Life is too short to ask more than twenty or so, but the results of my little inquiry are suggestive. It is unlikely that

Eats, Shoots and Leaves—or any such personal account—would ever be used systematically as a real guide to usage. It could hardly act as a textbook, given its anecdotal and selective character; but it is an enticing read, so perhaps some people are indeed trying to use it in that way. If it succeeds in helping them improve their punctuational practice, that's marvellous. If it succeeds only in increasing their intolerance levels, that's depressing.

The jury will be out for a while yet. I fear it has already done some damage. Which is a great shame, for that was not Lynne's intention at all.

22

Consequences

THE previous two chapters raise a couple of rather important questions. Why is punctuation so difficult? Why is it so variable? You wouldn't think a system which, after all, contains only a couple of dozen marks would be such a problem.

The reason is that we are trying to make punctuation do two jobs at once. Two incompatible jobs. We are using it to reflect the sound of the voice; and we are using it to organize grammar.

Punctuation began, as we have seen in the previous chapter, as an attempt to write down the inflections of the voice. If the preacher wanted a reminder that there should be a pause, or that his voice should go up or down, then the easiest way to do it was to make a mark on the page.

By degrees, this sonic function of punctuation became more complex. Today, several punctuation marks tell us how we should inflect our voices. A question mark tells us to be questioning? Yes, it does. An exclamation mark tells us to be exclamatory! (Two facing parentheses tell us to drop our voice when reading the intervening content.) An <u>underline</u>

or *italics* or (on screen) a pair of *asterisks* tells us to emphasize something.

Sometimes, contrasting punctuation marks signal a clear difference in meaning which reflects the different ways in which we can say a sentence. How would you say these two sentences?

The eggs are in the fridge, aren't they?
The eggs are in the fridge, aren't they!

The first one is 'asking': I do not know that the eggs are in the fridge, and I want you to inform me. The second one is 'telling': you should already know that the eggs are in the fridge. Don't be so stupid. In speech, the contrast is signalled by the intonation of the voice. In writing, punctuation does the job.

But punctuation does something which intonation does not do. I can say these sentences in such a way that you do not know whether I am asking or telling. Indeed, you might say: 'Are you asking me or telling me?' In writing, however, the distinction is clear-cut. There is no intermediate punctuation mark between ! and ?.

This is one of the problems. Punctuation makes us think in black-and-white terms, whereas speech does not. It forces us to make distinctions, where speech does not. We have to show a sentence coming to an end in writing. We don't have to do it in speech. If you don't believe me, record a piece of informal conversation and then try transcribing it. You will find it very difficult to identify where the sentences end.

Speech is inevitably more fluid and dynamic than writing, but it doesn't usually cause any problems because of what in Chapter 4 I called 'simultaneous feedback'. In a conversation, if I'm unclear, you can ask me about it. You can't do this if I'm writing. Even on screen, there's a delay between when I write and when you respond - though instant messaging is reducing that delay to a minimum. And most written messages don't get any response at all.

In short, writing is autonomous in a way that speech is not. That's why we have to take such care. If I write something that is ambiguous or incoherent, I have to live with it. It is there, on the page. And one of the main means of ensuring that my writing is neither ambiguous nor incoherent is punctuation.

But now a second issue arises. Most punctuation marks have little or no sonic value at all—notwithstanding the attempts of writers such as Lindley Murray to give them one (Chapter 21). It is not the case that a full stop always correlates with a pause beat, or is always twice the length of a comma, and so on. People who try to impose such systems never agree about what the lengths should be. And they certainly aren't performable.

Punctuation exists not only to reflect speech. It exists to make sense of writing. Even though writing developed centuries ago as a way of writing down speech, it has evolved as a medium with distinctive properties of its own. There are things we can do in writing that can never be done in speech. Think of type size, typefaces, colour, movement (on screen), and all the visual impact of calligraphy.

Think also of the visual distinctions between chapters, sections, and paragraphs. Think of distinctions such as the following:

This is a Very Important Point.

Or the way Christopher Robin reacts to Winnie the Pooh's suggestion:

'We might go in your umbrella,' said Pooh.
'?'
'We might go in your umbrella,' said Pooh.
'!!!!!!'
For suddenly Christopher Robin saw that they might.

Try saying that aloud.

Writing is a very different medium from speech, and it has different consequences. When we write, ambiguities arise that we would never dream of in speech, simply because writing is not up to capturing all the nuances of the spoken language. When we speak, we unselfconsciously make distinctions that are quite tricky to implement in writing. For instance, consider the following scenario.

Jane has one brother and he lives abroad and he has written her a letter. Mary has more than one brother, only one of whom lives abroad, and he has written her a letter. Without any punctuation at all, each of the girls could tell us this:

my brother who's abroad has written to me

But this is ambiguous. How are we to make the distinction?

This was one of the rules that grammarians introduced when they tried to bring punctuation under control.

They noticed that, in making this distinction in speech, Mary's version keeps the first four words as a single rhythm unit—my-brother-who's-abroad—whereas Jane's uses two rhythm units—my-brother / who's-abroad. And they showed this by the use of commas:

> My brother who's abroad has written to me. (Mary's meaning)
> My brother, who's abroad, has written to me. (Jane's meaning)

In trying to describe this distinction, unfortunately, they then lost most of us. Being grammarians, they brought in terminology. *Who's abroad* they called a relative clause. So far, so good. Now, Jane has only one brother. The fact that he is abroad just happens to be the case. She could have left this bit out, and her sentence would have the same meaning:

> My brother has written to me.

The relative clause doesn't define or restrict the meaning of *brother* in any way. Some grammarians called this 'non-defining'. Others called it 'non-restrictive'. They meant the same thing.

By contrast, Mary has more than one brother. The fact that he's abroad is critical to deciding which brother has written the letter. Mary's other brother(s) at home evidently haven't been writing to her. She can't leave that bit out without crucially altering the meaning. Here the relative clause *does* define or restrict the meaning of *brother*. It is 'defining' or 'restrictive'. Both terms are used.

That is why poor Lynne Truss got beaten up by the *New Yorker* reviewer (Chapter 20). Her book dedication reads:

> To the memory of the striking Bolshevik printers of St Petersburg who, in 1905, demanded to be paid the same rate for punctuation marks as for letters, and thereby directly precipitated the first Russian Revolution

The reviewer was technically right, as we can see if we reduce this sentence to its essentials.

First, we need to remove *in 1905*, which has a pair of parenthetical commas, and get rid of the descriptive bits. We are left with:

> To the memory of the printers who demanded to be paid.

The absence of a comma suggests that this is like Mary's brother. This is a book remembering those printers who demanded to be paid. It suggests that there were other printers who did not demand to be paid. But Lynne—presumably (I do not know this story)—did not mean this. She meant that *all* the printers demanded to be paid. She should, said the reviewer, have inserted the comma after *St Petersburg* to show that she had a non-restrictive meaning in mind. It's a howler, said the reviewer—and in a book on punctuation, too.

Well, up to a point, Lord Copper. Admittedly, Lynne has got herself into trouble by surrounding her *in 1905* by commas. Plainly, she wanted to express a distinctive rhythm. And, having done that, if she wanted to express the non-restrictive meaning, she would need to have used three commas in a row.

> To the memory of the striking Bolshevik printers of St Petersburg, who, in *1905*, demanded

Most people would find that overkill. Too many commas make a text very difficult to read.

Do you see the fundamental reason for the difficulty? The two commas surrounding *in 1905* are there to express the sound-effect of this part of the sentence. The comma after *printers* is there to express a grammatical contrast. We need all three, if we want to do both. But if we put all three in, then suddenly the sentence starts to look cluttered.

I don't know how conscious of this issue Lynne was when she composed the dedication. Evidently the phonetic criterion was foremost in her mind. But if she wanted to defend her choice against the *New Yorker* reviewer, she could do so by relying on a very important criterion: context.

All Lynne has to say is that the meaning of her dedication is clear from the context, whether we use commas or not. Only sticklers would insist on making the distinction when it isn't necessary. The *New Yorker* reviewer was evidently a stickler. But then, by her own admission, so is Lynne. 'Hoist by your own petard' comes to mind.

23

Context

ONTEXT is the one big thing that prescriptive writers never take into account. Yet it is crucial. It applies to everything—sounds, spellings, punctuation, grammar, vocabulary. And it is the one thing that is most often ignored.

Probably the best example of ignoring context is all the hoo-ha surrounding the so-called 'dangling participle'. Here's an example, from a recent book on usage. John Humphrys heard this on the radio:

> Driving in from the airport, the flags were fluttering proudly.

He comments:

> What accomplished flags they must have been.

But no one in a million years would interpret that sentence wrongly. It is not ambiguous for the obvious reason that we all know that flags don't drive. The context makes it perfectly clear. Only someone who has been taught wrongly—brought up to believe that dangling participles are *always* a problem— would make the mistake of ignoring context.

Here, as in earlier chapters, we see a good idea going horribly wrong. There are indeed many cases where we need to be alert to the possibility of ambiguity. John's book gives an excellent example of such a case:

Surrounded by barbed wire, armed soldiers guarded the prisoners from watchtowers.

Who was surrounded by barbed wire? This isn't like the flags example, because we know that anyone can be surrounded by barbed wire. Our knowledge of life will suggest to us that it has to be the prisoners. But it *could* be the guards. Either way, it makes us uncertain what the writer meant, and that certainly goes against the need for clarity. We would be well advised to rephrase, in such cases. For example:

Armed soldiers in watchtowers guarded the prisoners, who were surrounded by barbed wire.

But just because there are some cases where there *is* ambiguity is no reason for looking for ambiguity where it does not exist. It is another illustration of the prescriptive grammarians losing the plot. They perceptively noticed a real problem of clarity, in some sentences, and then, in their obsession with bringing the language under total control, so that there are never any exceptions, tried to convince us that there is always a problem. And for 250 years the brainwashing succeeded.

Intelligent people, sensitive to the way language works, will not be fooled for ever. You cannot put language in a cage, keep it separate from real life. Language exists to enable us to think and talk about life. Life is messy. We think complex thoughts. So therefore language is messy and complex. The rules take us so far and then peter out. But we are able to carry on using language successfully, even when the rules are uncertain or have exceptions, because we can call on our knowledge of the world to help us. Knowledge is more powerful than language. Whatever prescriptive grammarians might say, we know that flags don't drive cars. We can rely on that.

It is the same with punctuation. We don't actually need it, most of the time, as the unpunctuated example in Chapter 21 illustrates. But, now that we have it, it is an enormous help to producing clarity of expression in writing and smooth comprehension in reading. Yet it will never solve all our problems of clarity. A couple of dozen marks can never be given such responsibility. There are always going to be problem cases.

That is what a good linguistically based grounding in punctuation should provide. It should give students a solid understanding of what the rules are—insofar as there *are* rules—and point out the difficulties in applying them. It should draw attention to the limitations of the punctuation system as a whole, and provide ideas about how to make good those limitations. One way is to read a lot, at the same time analysing how experienced authors solve the problem. Another is to write a lot, in different contexts, at the same time analysing the differences that punctuation marks make.

This is the kind of thing that is increasingly taking place now in schools in the UK, thanks to the National Curriculum in English. It has taken a while to build up steam, since the new system was introduced in the early 1990s. You can't reverse a period of linguistic barrenness overnight. For one thing, teachers have to be trained—teachers who themselves missed out on the kind of training they are now expected to put into practice. Textbooks have to be written, and that takes time. There still aren't enough good teaching materials around. But enormous progress has been made, as we shall see in Chapter 30.

Most language pundits have no idea that such good language work is taking place in schools these days. John Humphrys is ten years out of date when he writes, in his introduction:

> It worries me that children do not get the same help that I had more than half a century ago. I wish the basic rules of grammar were still taught to every child.

His wish has already come true—but with a difference. The help is much better. Teachers spend a lot of time explaining about rules, and not just imposing them. And examiners will only give marks if these explanations are understood.

But none of this helps people who were educated in that barren period—a forty-year wilderness which lasted roughly from 1960 to 2000. Most of them had little or no training in the formal properties of language. They would know such properties existed, because they would hear people talking about them. Split infinitives, prepositions, dangling participles. Moreover, the people talking about them were older than they were. They were their bosses. And these bosses seemed to know what they were talking about. They talked with such authority. Really, Smith, another split infinitive? Don't you know anything, lad?

For 'lad' read 'lass'. For 'Smith' read any name. Everyone in this age group felt inferior, faced with such apparent knowledge. The fact that much of this knowledge was spurious would never have occurred to them. You can only argue against quackery by using evidence, which means knowledge, and they had none. So they tried to improve themselves, turning to books which claimed to solve all problems. Or turning to courses. The face began to appear in newspapers, looking out at them accusingly. 'Are YOU shamed by your mistakes in English?'

If enough people tell you you are making mistakes, you begin to believe it. And because people do make mistakes, some of the time, it fuels the feeling of insecurity. Panic, even. If even Shakespeare gets it wrong (Chapter 13), what chance have I got?

So no wonder people feel they need help. No wonder they look for a book. And no wonder that they should choose Lynne's, which is so elegantly written. But they wouldn't have done this if they had been taught well in the first place. And the reason they weren't taught well is that they weren't taught about the structure of language at all.

So, will reading Lynne's book—or any usage manual—help? Unfortunately not.

Reading a book on usage is an attempt at 'Do it yourself' linguistics. It is bound to fail, because it is too late.

Linguistic education needs to take place while we are young. That's when we can find the time, resources, and help. Very rarely do people get all three when they are older. Learning a language—mother-tongue or foreign—is a long and complex exercise. It needs a steady and systematic approach. It certainly can't be reduced to a few succinct points in alphabetical order in a usage manual.

If usage manuals lived up to their promises, we would be home and dry by now. The Dean of Canterbury, Henry Alford, published his usage manual in 1860: *The Queen's English*. The Fowler brothers published theirs in 1906: *The King's English*. A century later and we can see the corpses of usage manuals littering the battlefields of English—Gowers and Partridge in the UK, Strunk and Levin in the USA. If any one of these had worked, we would not have needed the others.

I am not against usage books, as such. I have written one myself. All I am saying is that they are not a panacea. They do not solve the underlying problem of obtaining systematic help about language. But they do have a value. They help to alert us to the issues of change that worry the more conservatively minded members of society. They also perform a valuable service in drawing attention to those features of language where it is all too easy to be lazy or careless, and where sense or intelligibility suffers as a result. And above all, in some recent books, they identify some serious problems of communication in contemporary society.

John Humphrys' *Lost for Words* is an excellent example. There is a maturity about his approach, born of a lifetime of listening to the waffle and doublespeak of politicians and pundits, and his targets need attacking. I hate doublespeak as much as he does. I have problems in decoding bureaucraticspeak, just as he does. His humour adds to the power of his approach. I loved the second half of his book.

The first half deals with a different world—a world full of the sort of grammatical issues that we have seen can be traced back to Lowth and Murray (Chapter 17). He gives many examples of his likes and dislikes. He is very worried about declining standards. He asserts, as did Sprat and Murray before him, that clarity is all. Good English, he says, is 'clear, simple, plain, and unambiguous'.

The logic of the book goes awry when he tries to link these two worlds. He thinks there is somehow a correlation between what happens in political doublespeak and the rules of grammar which upset him so much. He seems to identify 'manipulating' with 'mangling'—by which he means not following the old grammatical rules. But there is no such correlation. Politicians can manipulate language while still following every rule in a prescriptive grammar. Conversely, people can break all those rules and yet be honest and direct. There is no causal relationship between prepositional manipulation and thought manipulation, any more than there is between splitting infinitives and splitting skulls.

John's approach would be even more effective, to my mind, if it became just that little bit more linguistically aware. I don't mean to sound patronizing. He says himself that he has no academic qualifications in the subject of language.

No reason why he should have, to do what he needs to do. But he needs to see that he is making connections where there aren't any. You won't find examples of 'bad grammar', in his sense, in the second half of his book. As soon as he attacks his real targets, he switches from grammar to vocabulary, and hits out at clichés and jargon. That is indeed where problems lie. Not in grammar.

But I am happy to live with his tastes in grammar, because his heart is definitely in the right place. He knows he is exaggerating when he satirizes teenage grunting. He says so. He doesn't like split infinitives, but he knows it is a 'bogus rule'. He likes end-placed prepositions and sentences beginning with conjunctions, but he knows that others don't share his tastes. He wants beauty, but he knows it is in the eye of the beholder. He is against extreme pedantry, calling it a 'virus'. So am I. He knows that 'usage is the final arbiter'. So do I. He applauds variety. 'Uniformity breeds sterility,' he says. Fantastic. I wish I'd said that.

If I had him in my class—if I had one so early in the morning—I would try to persuade him that he worries too much about the placing of *only*, for context sorts out most of the imagined problems. Not all. Most. And in speech we are dealing with a different linguistic world from the one we see in writing. He picks up his 4-year-old and gives him a special cuddle because the kiddy said *I'm going to take only one* [dinosaur to school]. I hope he gave him another cuddle when the child learned an even more subtle rule, that in speech *only* relates in meaning to the following most strongly stressed word (as illustrated in Chapter 19).

I would try to get him not to worry so much about the overlap of meaning between *less* and *fewer*—one of the points that prescriptive grammarians turned into a big issue. Meaning is never at risk in such a case. I would try to get him not to worry so much about such modern uses as *almost unique* and *I'm good*. He shouldn't need to. He says at one point, 'if something expands our power of expression it is good'. Well, then, he should be welcoming *almost unique*, which is helping us to make a subtle distinction— a state of affairs which is approaching uniqueness but which has not yet reached it. And *I'm good*, in answer to 'How are you?', now allows us to focus on our general state of mind, instead of just on our health, which is all that *I'm well* allowed us to do.

I'd also try to get him not to worry so much about some of the pronunciation trends he dislikes. He doesn't like the way stress is shifting in such words as <u>research</u>. He doesn't like the way young people lift their voices at the ends of statements. More on this in Chapter 26.

And I'd try to get him not to worry so much about the way words narrow their meaning over time. He cites the footballer's *We got a result*, where *result* means 'win'. He cites the weather-forecaster's *There's an awful lot of weather about today*, where *weather* means 'bad weather'. This has happened thousands of times in the history of English. *Meat* in Old English meant 'food'; now it means just one kind of food. *Umpire* in Shakespeare meant 'arbitrator'; now it means just one kind of arbitrator—in games and contests.

On the other hand, I wouldn't stop him worrying about the trends which are causing a loss of ability to use standard English spelling. He cites *I could of gone*. This is a basic spelling error, inspired by the phonetic identity between *of* and *'ve* (*have*). Teachers need to alert children to these false friends. Spelling rules are the clearest indicators of standard English, so they need special attention (Chapter 24). But if the teaching is failing, we need to find out why and do something about it. It isn't just the kids who should shoulder the blame.

Why would I work on John Humphrys in this way? Because these points are distracting him—and therefore us—from the Bigger Issues. If he hadn't devoted so much space to his worries over what are often non-worries, then he would have had more space to keep attacking things that are much more important.

It's a pity, because John Humphrys illustrates a new genre of usage publishing. So does Lynne Truss. It is a genre which is characterized by humour—a characteristic notably lacking in prescriptive writers. You have to look hard to find a vestige of a smile in Johnson, Lowth, Murray, Fowler, and all the others. They are all being too angry to laugh. John and Lynne show us how you can be angry and laugh at the same time. It's a healthy sign. The rhetoric of zero tolerance aside, they make me empathize with what they have to say. I cannot empathize much with the earlier writers. That is why I call one group, rather than the other, by their first names.

24

Spelling

W HAT had been happening to spelling, all this while? We left it in Chapter 5, beginning to settle down after a period when the spelling reformers had sunk their teeth into it, tried to sort it out, and failed. That was during the sixteenth century.

There was still a huge amount of spelling variation a generation or so later, in Shakespeare's time. The First Folio contains *accused*, *accusde*, and *accust*, as well as abbreviated *accus'd*. *Adieu* is spelled *adieu*, *adew*, *adiew*, and *adue*. Doubtless the manuscripts were even more varied. I took a sample of 100 words beginning with A from the First Folio. They displayed 180 variant forms, and 53 of them were different from those in use today. That's one in three. In 1623, a spelling standard was still some way off.

By the end of the seventeenth century, when Dryden was writing, the figure had fallen to about one in fifty words. The first weekly newspapers, the writing of John Milton, and the pamphleteering of the Civil War had exercised considerable influence. Many of the remaining differences were due to the penchant for abbreviating words, such as *admir'd* and *blam'd*; but we also find such forms as *custome*, *daies* (days), *drest* (dressed), *errours*, *every where*, *extreamly*, *farr*, *justifie*, *gayety*, *mistriss*, *preheminence*, and *unaffraid*.

A century later, and the figure had fallen to about 1 in 400 words. Most of the words defined in Johnson's *Dictionary* are spelled the same as today, but you will notice *fewel* (fuel), *raindeer*, *villany*, *wellmet*, and a few more. The choice between final -*l* and -*ll* was still in a state of flux: we find *downfal* but *pitfall*, *petrol* but *comptroll*. So was the choice between -*or* and -*our*: we find *confessor* and *inheritor* alongside *oratour* and *possessour*.

The main difference is the way words ending in -*c* are spelled. Johnson asserts at one point:

The English never use *c* at the end of a word.

And indeed, throughout his book we find *acrostick*, *antick*, *comick*, and many more. But, fifty years later, this rule had been replaced by the modern one.

In 1755, when Johnson published his *Dictionary*, English spelling seemed to be on track to becoming the primary marker of standard English. The notion of 'correct spelling' seemed altogether more trustworthy than correct grammar, vocabulary, or punctuation. This was a huge change in attitude. Correct spelling was not something which had much bothered people before. In Shakespeare's day you could spell your name in different ways and nobody seemed to mind. But not in the eighteenth century. Lord Chesterfield was one who gave his son a good telling off:

You spell induce, *enduce*; and grandeur, you spell grand*ure*; two faults, of which few of my house-maids would have been guilty. I must tell you, that orthography, in the true sense of the word, is so absolutely necessary for a man of letters, or a gentleman, that one false spelling may fix a ridicule upon him for the rest of his life; and I know a man of quality, who never recovered the ridicule of having spelled *wholesome* without the *w*.

Johnson's work seemed to consolidate English spelling as never before. He was well aware of the problem presented by alternative spellings, and so he regularly drew attention to cases where such alternatives existed. He would often make recommendations as to which one should be used, and his influence undoubtedly made some of them permanent, such as the distinction between *travel* and *travail*. But within twenty-five years of his death, something happened which would change everything. The arrival of American English.

Noah Webster was born in West Hartford, Connecticut, in 1758, and worked as a teacher, clerk, and lawyer. Early on he became dissatisfied with the lack of an American perspective in the texts he had to use. 'Nothing can be more ridiculous', he says, 'than a servile imitation of the manners, the language, and the vices of foreigners.' He would in due course publish a dictionary, a grammar, and a guide to spelling, and his work made him a household name in America, comparable in stature to Dr Johnson in Britain.

Spelling, he felt, was the heart of the matter. He observes:

a difference between the English orthography and the American… is an object of vast political consequence.

So he initiated what turned out to be the only successful English spelling reform of modern times. In his *Compendious Dictionary* of 1806 he outlined two main principles. One was 'the omission of all superfluous and silent letters'. The other was the 'substitution of a character that has a certain definite sound, for one that is more vague and indeterminate'.

By no means all of his suggestions caught on. Many final -*e*'s (as in *definite*) and 'silent' vowels (as in *feather*) stayed in American English. On the other hand, he was successful in changing -*re* words to -*er* (*center*) and omitting *u* from words ending in -*our* (*color*). Today, most of the differences between American and British spelling are due to the American words having fewer letters—in two-thirds of cases, one vowel instead of two, as these examples illustrate:

US	UK
anemic	anaemic
armor	armour
caldron	cauldron
diarrhea	diarrhoea
smolder	smoulder

or no vowel at all:

ax	axe
catalog	catalogue
largess	largesse

Consonant changes included the use of -*z*- for -*s*- in verb endings (*advertize*, *analyze*), replacing -*ce* by -*se* (*defense*, *offense*), the dropping of a final -*k* from words ending in -*ick* (*musick*, *physick*—something that was also happening in Britain), and simplifying the double consonant before a suffix (*traveling*, *appareled*). A number of other changes can be seen in this next selection:

US	UK	US	UK
check	cheque	program	programme
donut	doughnut	maneuver	manoeuvre
draftsman	draughtsman	plow	plough
curb	kerb	pajamas	pyjamas
jail	gaol	tire	tyre

Most of the changes were rejected out of hand in Britain as being 'American' and condemned with considerable emotion. As a result, they stayed firmly on the US side of the Atlantic—at least, until a twentieth-century wave of borrowing changed the situation.

It was the beginning of a new era of usage, as far as spelling was concerned. The differences between British and American spelling grew, during the nineteenth century, as scientific vocabulary increased. Thousands of new words in the various domains of science came to be spelled differently, such as those beginning with *archae-* or *arche-* (*archaeopteryx*), *haem-* or *hem-* (*haemoglobin*), and *paed-* or *ped-* (*paediatric*). And in the twentieth century, there were further complications when American and British spellings began to turn up variously around the world, depending on the respective influence of the two countries. We find

British spelling in Hong Kong, but American spelling in the Philippines. We find a mixture of both systems in Canada.

In 1986, a professor of English at London University, Sidney Greenbaum, carried out a survey to estimate just how much spelling variation there was in Modern English. He took a medium-size (1,690-page) desk dictionary, and identified all the words spelled in more than one way under the letter *A*. He found an average of three variant forms per page—296 entries. Extrapolating from this to the dictionary as a whole, he estimated there would be nearly 5,000 variants altogether. As a percentage of all the entries in the dictionary, this was a remarkable 5.6 per cent. Greenbaum stopped there. But if we extend his approach, we get even more remarkable results.

If we include the spelling variation found in more specialized scientific and technical words, his figure greatly increases—to around 14 per cent. It goes much higher if we add all the variations we see today because of the influence of American spelling on British practice—such as the often encountered -z- for -s- in such words as *atomize, atomizer, atomizable, atomization*. On top of that, there are all the variations in hyphenation and capitalization, which I referred to when talking about punctuation (Chapter 21). Today we will find both *Bible* and *bible*, *Moon* and *moon*, *dark room* and *dark-room* and *darkroom*.

If we widen our net still further, to include all the proper names of encyclopedic inquiry, the figure will rise again.

Think of all the transliteration differences that exist in working with foreign languages. Is it *Tutankhamen*, *Tut'ankhamun*, *Tutankamen*, or a hyphenated version reflecting the structure of the original language, such as *Tut-ankh-amun*?

How many words have variant spellings in present-day English? The above calculations are based only on samples, but the true figure cannot be much less than 25 per cent. The notion of a 'standard' spelling system therefore needs to be taken with a huge pinch of salt, when perhaps a quarter of the words in the dictionary and encyclopedia have alternative forms.

The turn of the nineteenth century saw the beginning, as well as the beginning of the end, of the dream of a totally standard English. In the eighteenth century, for just a few decades, a genuinely universal standard did exist, assiduously constructed by a team of linguistic master-builders— Johnson, Murray, and the others. But American English drove a Wells Fargo coach and horses through the idea that a single monolithic variety of English could be used throughout the educated English-using world.

Nor was the variation the result of American English alone. Differences such as *Moon* and *moon* or *dark-room* and *darkroom* are nothing to do with regional origins. Forms such as *judg(e)ment* are used on both sides of the Atlantic. And the arrival of the Internet has begun to further eliminate the identity divide. When a page in English arrives on your screen today, it might have originated in Britain, America, or any other English-speaking source. We are being presented with spelling variation on a world scale, with no easy way of deciding which variant belongs where. And the technology itself adds further variants, such as dropping accents (*cliche*, *cafe*) and promoting the use of new forms (as in text messaging).

It is unclear what will happen. On the one hand, the Internet is increasing the amount of variation. On the other, by exposing us all to the same variation, it is making us familiar with it, and eventually new standards could emerge. Certain spellings will very likely come to be preferred in due course. Internet users vote with their fingers.

So where does this leave us today, as far as 'correct spelling' is concerned? We can take comfort from the fact that at least three-quarters of the words in English display no variation, even on the Internet. That situation is immensely better than it was in the age of Shakespeare. There is a large core of orthographic stability, whose mastery remains a sign of educated prowess. But there is no escaping the fact that a totally uniform spelling system does not exist in English. History suggests that perhaps it never will.

None of this helps beleaguered English teachers, who have to work out ways of managing the variations and changes that exist, and devising interesting ways of present-ing the facts to their students. Nor does it make the task of those wishing to master English spelling any easier. The situation hasn't been helped by a veritable dearth of good analyses and presentations of the spelling system. Who will be the Lynne Truss of spelling, I wonder?

25

Elocution

WHAT had been happening to pronunciation, all this while? We left it in Chapter 12, where we saw the eighteenth-century writers becoming increasingly concerned about the new regional accents and dialects that were emerging in English. If standards were emerging in spelling, punctuation, grammar, and vocabulary, then surely it was going to be possible to have a standard for pronunciation too. The only question was: where was it to be found?

Dr Johnson had been particularly worried about pronunciation. He despaired of ever being able to handle it, because he knew that English had a 'double pronunciation; one, cursory and colloquial; the other, regular and solemn'. It was a distinction which we can trace right back to the Middle Ages (Chapter 2). No chance of ever being able to handle colloquial speech, he thought, because of the way it was 'made different, in different mouths, by negligence, unskilfulness, or affectation'. Trying to capture this kind of pronunciation, he says in his preface, is like trying 'to enchain syllables, and to lash the wind'.

But lexicography is all about trying to capture a language and get it down on a page, so Johnson had to do something. He therefore decided to represent the solemn variety, and took the written language as a guide:

> For pronunciation the best general rule is, to consider those as the most elegant speakers who deviate least from the written words.

Lindley Murray made the same point, when recommending the pronunciation of verb-forms ending with -*ing*:

> it is a good rule, with respect to pronunciation, to adhere to the written words, unless custom has clearly decided otherwise.

The principle is much older than Johnson and Murray. We can see it operating in the sixteenth century, when the spelling reformers were at work. Thomas Elyot is quite clear about what should be done linguistically to a nobleman's son before he is 7. The nurses and other women about him should ensure

> that they speke none englisshe but that which is cleane, polite, perfectly and articulately pronounced, omittinge no lettre or sillable, as folisshe women often times do of a wantonnesse, wherby diuers noble men and gentilmennes chyldren, (as I do at this daye knowe), haue attained corrupte and foule pronuntiation.

Omitting no letter or syllable? That seems like a very strong criterion. Did he mean pronouncing even 'silent letters'? It seems, yes. There were pedants who insisted on pronouncing absolutely everything, even the letters which had been added to a word to show their etymology. Shakespeare was one of the first to poke fun at them, when he displays Holofernes' shock at the way Don Armado pronounces his words (in *Love's Labour's Lost*, v. i. 17):

> I abhor such fanatical phantasims [extravagantly behaved person], such insociable and point-device [affectedly precise] companions, such rackers of orthography as to speak 'dout', sine [without] 'b', when he should say 'doubt'; 'det' when he should pronounce 'debt'—'d, e, b, t', not 'd, e, t'.

This is how many people think of pronunciation usage today. They feel that they should pronounce the *t* in *often* 'because it is there in the spelling'. And they dismiss the pronunciation of *singin'* because it 'drops the *g*'. 'Spelling pronunciations', as they are called, sometimes catch on: we now say *waistcoat* and *forehead*, not *weskit* and *forrid* (except in the nursery rhyme, where it rhymes with *horrid*). A list of the 'most mispronounced words in English' will contain several that are thought to be wrong because they do not sound out every letter, such as *February*, *library*, *Antarctic* (pronounce the *c*), and *miniature* (pronounce the *a*).

Follow the writing. You might think that this was enough to guarantee a standard pronunciation. But it was not enough for John Walker, who follows in the footsteps of George Puttenham and others, 200 years before (Chapter 7).

Walker was to pronunciation what Johnson was to vocabulary and Murray to grammar. Indeed, after the publication of his magnum opus in 1791, people started calling him 'Elocution Walker'—just as Johnson had been called 'Dictionary Johnson' some years before. The book's impressive title reads as follows:

A Critical Pronouncing Dictionary and Expositor of the English Language: to which are prefixed, Principles of English Pronunciation: Rules to be Observed by the Natives of Scotland, Ireland, and London, for Avoiding their Respective Peculiarities; and Directions to Foreigners for Acquiring a Knowledge of the Use of this Dictionary. The Whole Interspersed with Observations Etymological, Critical, and Grammatical.

It had over a hundred editions.

Walker knows where the best model of pronunciation is to be found. Where else but in the capital?

though the pronunciation of London is certainly erroneous in many words, yet, upon being compared with that of any other place, it is undoubtedly the best; that is, not only the best by courtesy, and because it happens to be the pronunciation of the capital, but the best by a better title—that of being more generally received.

'Received'—an early use of a term which would become a dominant feature of later pronunciation studies. He means 'received among the learned and polite'—the cultured society which made up the universities, the court, and their associated social structure.

What about everyone else? Walker sees them as inhabiting a pronunciation wilderness.

the great bulk of the nation, and those who form the most important part in it, are without these advantages, and therefore want such a guide to direct them as is here offered.

The further away they live, the worse their situation:

> harsh as the sentence may seem, those at a considerable distance from the capital, do not only mispronounce many words taken separately, but they scarcely pronounce, with purity, a single word, syllable, or letter.

And that means the Scots and the Irish are in the worst danger of all, which is why they receive special mention in the subtitle to his book.

Walker is particularly hard on the Cockney speakers in London, who also get a mention in his title. He gives a particular reason for this: Cockney is in an especially bad position, as it is so close to the court and the city. Because 'people of education in London are generally free from the vices of the vulgar', they notice Cockney more. It may have fewer faults than are found in provincial dialects, but it is always to be heard, thrusting itself harshly into the ears of the polite. As a consequence:

> the vulgar pronunciation of London, though not half so erroneous as that of Scotland, Ireland, or any of the provinces, is, to a person of correct taste, a thousand times more offensive and disgusting.

For anyone who felt threatened by such a powerful attack— which meant most people in the country—there was a way forward: elocution. Thomas Sheridan, the father of the playwright, was famous for his countrywide lectures on elocution, speaking to packed halls. John Watkins, the editor of Richard Brinsley Sheridan's memoirs, reflects on the 'incredible' success of his courses—'upwards of sixteen hundred subscribers, at a guinea each, besides occasional visitors'. Copies of his book, *A Course of Lectures on Elocution* (1763), sold at half a guinea each.

Let's just reflect on that for a moment. Translated into modern values, that is equivalent to a course fee per person of about £75. In today's money, one of Sheridan's courses must have brought him in well over £150,000. Elocution was big business, and people were prepared to pay for it. It would have cost an up-and-coming clerk a quarter of his weekly salary to attend one of Sheridan's courses. But that is what the members of the new middle class did. A course of elocution was a good career move.

After Sheridan and Walker, people increasingly began to talk about the desirability of 'taking the edges off their accent' or 'losing their accent altogether'. Then they started to say that they had 'no accent'. Everyone has an accent, of course, even those who think they haven't one. What they meant was that they had—or wanted—no detectable regional accent.

Walker's prescriptive temperament plainly reflects the mindset which we have seen to be a defining feature of the eighteenth century. He did not believe in the desirability of linguistic change and he was totally against words being pronounced in different ways. 'A diversity of pronunciation', he says in his preface, 'is at once so ridiculous and embarrassing.'

Sheridan took the same line, in *A Dissertation on the Causes of Difficulties, Which Occur, in Learning the English Tongue:*

> The consequence of teaching children by one method, and one uniform system of rules, would be an uniformity of pronunciation in all so instructed. Thus might the rising generation, born and bred in different Countries and Counties, no longer have a variety of dialects, but as subjects of one King, have one common tongue.

Today, at least 96 per cent of the population of the British Isles speak with an identifiable regional accent. The figure would have been even higher in the eighteenth century. Sheridan and Walker were making an awful lot of people feel inferior, by their stance. But they, of course, would have taken that remark as a plaudit, not a criticism.

26

Pronunciation

A T the beginning of the nineteenth century, pronunciation still had some way to go to reach its present-day character. We know this because writers say more about the way words were pronounced, during that century, than ever before. Then, in the last few decades of the century, there was the magic moment. The first cylinder recordings of speech came to be made. In London's Science Museum, you can actually hear Florence Nightingale talking.

There is a surprising amount of phonetic anecdote reported in the nineteenth century. People wrote about the speech patterns they remembered from an earlier generation. We find them talking about the pronunciation of *oblige* as *obleege*, *daughters* as *darters*, *gold* as *goold*, *seven* as *sivin*, and *china* as *chayney*, as well as many words where the stress pattern was different from what it is today, as in *compensate*, and *Trafalgar*.

Along with the changes come the complaints. In *Recollections of the Table-talk of Samuel Rogers*, published just after his death in 1855, we read:

> The now fashionable pronunciation of several words is to me at least very offensive: *cóntemplate*—is bad enough; but *bálcony* makes me sick.

He was upset because the pronunciation he was used to was *balcony*—bal-<u>coh</u>-nee. Today, of course, we can't understand what all the fuss was about. Everyone says <u>bal</u>*cony*. Instead, people claim that <u>research</u> makes them sick. And in fifty years' time it will be something else. Word stress in English ebbs and flows like the tide.

The favoured south-eastern accent didn't stand still. In 1791, John Walker affirmed that the 'best speakers' pronounced such words as *singing* without the final *g*, and echoes of this accent could be heard in upper-class speech in the early decades of the twentieth century (*huntin', shootin', fishin'*). Today, 'dropping the *g*' is usually condemned as a non-standard feature. It may be different in fifty years' time. Tide-flow again.

Probably the most important change during this period affected the pronunciation of *r* after a vowel. Present in English since Anglo-Saxon times, John Walker had already noted that it was weakening, referring to it as a 'soft' sound in words like *farm*. In the early 1800s we find rhymes and respellings suggesting that *r* after a vowel had actually disappeared: *harm* is said to rhyme with *calm*, and *alms* with *arms*. Also, when people wrote *calm* in a mock-phonetic way they sometimes spelled it *karm*. They would have spelled it *kahm*, or some such, if the *r* had continued to be sounded.

The perception that the language was 'losing a letter' was a cause of profound upset to some writers, who bitterly condemned poets who made use of what they called 'Cockney rhymes'. Keats, for example, rhymed *thoughts / sorts* and *thorns / fawns*, and was heavily censured for his pains.

Today, the controversy is in the other direction: the absence of *r* after a vowel is a standard feature of the prestige accent. It is the insertion of an *r* that attracts all the criticism. This is the infamous 'intrusive *r*'—the pronunciation of an *r* consonant to ease the transition between adjacent vowels.

Probably no feature of contemporary pronunciation has attracted more criticism than intrusive *r*. Examples include *Africa[r] and Asia*, *the idea[r] of it*, and *draw[r]ing*. The crucial point is that there is no letter *r* in the spelling. The usage may be as old as English, but it came to be noticed in the late eighteenth century, when it was condemned by those who felt that pronunciation should reflect writing as much as possible. Educated speakers were recommended to avoid it. Today, the usage continues to attract strong criticism. Some radio broadcasters, indeed, anxious to avoid irate letters from pedantic listeners, mark up their scripts in advance to identify any problem cases. *Law and order* they say, ever so carefully.

The nineteenth century also saw the emergence of the name by which the prestige accent is usually known today: it was said to be 'received'. This non-regional educated British accent has since been variously labelled an 'Oxford accent', a 'BBC accent', the 'King's/Queen's accent', and a 'public-school accent'. It did not exist at the end of the eighteenth century. On the contrary, features of regional pronunciation were a normal characteristic of educated speech.

A small number of key features identified the new accent, usually demonstrating a desire to distance speakers as far as possible from the way Cockneys talked. In particular, the letter *h* was to be sounded at the beginning of words—*hospital* not *'ospital*—and was not to be introduced if it was not there in the spelling (*my arm*, not *my harm*). The *t* in the middle of such words as *bottle* was to be pronounced, and not replaced by the glottal stop. The two *th* sounds (as in *thin* and *this*) were to be pronounced with the tongue between the teeth, and not replaced by an *f* or v.

There was never total uniformity, but this new accent was certainly much more supra-regional than any previous English accent had ever been. The regional neutrality was due to educated people from different geographical backgrounds increasingly coming into contact with and accommodating to each other's speech. Greater social mobility had brought urban and rural dwellers together. More universities brought people from different parts of the country together in one place. Schoolteachers were exercising an increased influence on their charges, and a momentum was building up within the schools themselves, especially in the private system.

The new accent eventually did come to be associated with a 'public-school education'—at such schools as Eton, Harrow, Winchester, and Westminster—followed by higher education at Oxford or Cambridge. And the accent then rapidly spread through the career-structure which such an education opened up—in the civil and diplomatic service (especially abroad, as the Empire expanded) and the Anglican Church. The immense pressure from the public-school system was probably the chief reason why the regional colouring of earlier educated speech largely died out between 1860 and 1890. By 1894 the philologist Richard Lloyd was able to talk about 'perfect' English as that which gives 'the least possible indication of local origin'.

It was because there was such a link with the public schools that when the phonetician Daniel Jones carried out his first description of the prestige accent, in 1917, he called it Public School Pronunciation:

> that most usually heard in everyday speech in the families of Southern English persons whose menfolk have been educated at the great public boarding schools.

He renamed it Received Pronunciation (RP) in 1926.

By then, of course, it had been further institutionalized by being adopted by the BBC. Lord Reith, the BBC's founder, expressed his policy in this way. 'It seemed desirable', he says,

> to adopt uniformity of principle and uniformity of pronunciation to be observed by Announcers with respect to doubtful words. The policy might be described as that of seeking a common denominator of educated speech.

The 'common denominator' was of course RP. And to help put this policy into practice, in 1926 the BBC appointed an Advisory Committee on Spoken English. It was chaired by the poet laureate, Robert Bridges, and included George Bernard Shaw, Daniel Jones, and A. Lloyd James. They made recommendations about variant forms, such as whether the *c* in *appreciation* should be pronounced as *s* or *sh*. The current Pronunciation Unit at the BBC still does.

But almost as soon as RP arrived, it began to fragment. It already contained a great deal of personal variation, and it was subject to change, like any other accent. By the beginning of the twentieth century it was displaying a range of chiefly age-related differences. Older speakers were said to be 'conservative'; young upper-class and professional people were called 'advanced'. Each group called the other 'affected'.

Then, during the 1960s, regional accents began to reassert themselves. RP retained its upper and upper-middle social-class connotation, as a supra-regional standard, but it slowly came to be affected by the growth of regional identities. Regional colouring, missing since the early nineteenth century, emerged once again. Phoneticians described the phenomenon as 'modified RP'. I am a good example. I speak a modified RP—a mixture of Welsh, Liverpudlian, and southern features, reflecting the three main parts of the country in which I have lived.

When I presented *English Now* on Radio 4 in the 1980s, listeners were always telling me off about it. One listener was so incensed that somebody should have been allowed to say *one* to rhyme with *don* rather than *done* that he wrote to the director-general about it. *And* he put a first-class stamp on the letter.

I never heard from the DG, but I did receive all the letters of complaint to the BBC in those days. My weekly programme was about English usage, and I think the people in charge of the post room at Broadcasting House were relieved to have somewhere to send them. They weren't just about pronunciation, of course, but about all aspects of grammar and vocabulary. They were almost always complaints. Only one in a hundred would praise anything. But they almost all put a first-class stamp on their letters. It wasn't enough for the letter to arrive eventually. It had to be there tomorrow. Time was running out for the language, you see. If Crystal was saying *one* as if it rhymed with *don*, this was an emergency. He needed to be stopped, and as quickly as possible.

But of course I was only one among thousands. In England, the range of the accent as spoken by the educated class has dramatically altered in recent years. It has especially incorporated a number of features previously associated with local London speech, resulting in the accent that the media have happily designated 'Estuary English'. This first came to public attention in the 1990s with reference to the accent emerging around the River Thames estuary. The label is hardly appropriate for a trend whose features can be heard as far north as Yorkshire and as far west as Dorset; but it seems to have stuck.

Estuary had been around for years before its name arrived. By the 1970s, accents showing a mixture of RP and Cockney were becoming noticeable. They were motivated by an upmarket movement of originally Cockney speakers and a downmarket trend towards 'ordinary' (as opposed to 'posh') speech by the middle class. By the 1990s, attitudes towards the new accent had begun to change. People started calling it 'warm', 'customer-friendly', and 'down to earth'. Then an amazing thing happened. RP began to attract some negative evaluations. People started calling it 'posh' and 'distant'. It was a remarkable turnaround.

For many people, no further evidence of the rehabilitation of regional accents is required than the voices heard at the ends of phones in call-centres throughout the UK, where Edinburgh Scots, Yorkshire, and other regional forms (including Indian English) are routinely encountered, but traditional RP hardly ever. The number of people using the old RP has fallen greatly. Estimates of usage in the 1980s were that between 3 and 5 per cent of the British population still used it—around two million. This must be now less than 2 per cent and falling.

Although the BBC held out until the 1970s against the use of regional colouring in the accents of its announcers, the eventual demise of the RP monopoly had been anticipated from the beginning. As early as 1926, the *Daily Chronicle* expressed its anxieties:

> Is there not some danger that the uniform system of training in pronunciation as well as voice production, which the B.B.C. is planning, may lead to a tiresome and possibly infectious monotony of utterance? We see no reason why the B.B.C. should not rather cultivate a variety of accent, intonation and blend of sound, so long as each variety is good of its kind.

Some twenty years later, broadcaster Wilfred Pickles made the same point in an eloquent defence of regional dialect:

> How terrible it is to think that we may some day lose that lovely soft Devonshire accent or the bluff and very wonderful Scots brogue or the amusing flatness and forthrightness of the

North-countryman's speech, or the music of the Welsh voice. May it be forbidden that we should ever speak like B.B.C. announcers, for our rich contrast of voices is a vocal tapestry of great beauty and incalculable value, handed down to us by our forefathers.

Pickles knew what happened when a regional voice disturbed the RP hegemony, because he had taken part in an experiment in the early part of the Second World War, when he had been asked to read the national news. According to the BBC announcer John Snagge, the Minister of Information had felt that Pickles's northern accent could be a useful security measure, because it 'might not be so easily copied by the Germans'. The decision caused headline news in the national press, with Pickles's 'short *a*' repeatedly picked upon: *Lahst a Thing of the Pahst* said one.

The BBC's Listener Research Department found Pickles's reading to be surprisingly popular, but a torrent of abuse came through the post. People complained that they were unable to believe the news when it was read in such an accent. Pickles enjoyed the fuss, but he eventually decided to give it up. He went 'up north' to Manchester, and carried on broadcasting from there.

There have been other famous cases of accent rejection. In 1937 Charles Chilton began to present a programme of popular music, but his 'cockney voice' led to his being taken off the air. Even as recently as 1980, some listeners to Radio 4 expressed anger over the Scottish accent of the presenter Susan Rae. I interviewed her about it in my *English Now* series. She was naturally distressed about it. And to the

BBC's eternal shame, she disappeared from the channel soon after.

She was perhaps the last casualty. The RP monopoly was already being slowly lowered into its coffin. In 1977 the Annan Report on the future of broadcasting had already commented: 'We welcome regional accents.' The rise of independent local broadcasting stations, basking in local speech, put the BBC under pressure to retain its share of the audience by doing likewise. Slowly, presenters began to display a few speech characteristics that would never have been heard in traditional RP.

Even some of the strongly stereotyped accents of the past, such as Welsh (Chapter 8), were rehabilitated. Huw Edwards began reading the main television evening news. Today, you would be hard pressed to find a weather-forecaster on television that didn't have regional colouring. For some reason that currently escapes me, this seems to be mainly Scottish.

And in December 2003, I experienced one of the most rewarding moments of all. I was driving down the M1 and turned on the 6 o'clock news. I recognized the voice straight away, back in the fold after too long an absence. It was Susan Rae.

27

Institutions

I N August 2005, the BBC did something I thought I would never see in my lifetime: it devoted a whole week to the celebration of regional accents and dialects.

I was closely involved from the outset, as I was asked to be the linguistic consultant in planning the event. One of the early meetings was at a very senior level in the BBC. Remembering the RP resonances of the organization in the past, I wasn't sure what to expect. But I felt very comfortable when I heard the Northern Irish voice of the BBC's Director of Nations and Regions, Pat Loughrey. And even more so when I met the man who was appointed the project director, Mick Ord, whose strong Liverpool accent brought me straight back to my own days in that city. Much of the detailed earlier planning had come out of the offices of the BBC in Cardiff, where Faith Mowbray represented a third regional strand.

On one marvellous day in Birmingham, programme-makers from all the BBC's regional radio stations gathered together to think up ways of handling the subject. It was one of the most creative days I have ever experienced. And, from an academic point of view, one of the most rewarding.

For *Voices Week* was not going to be an event just for broad-casters and listeners. A huge collection of high-quality audio recordings was envisaged, and these would be archived for analysis by dialect researchers. It would be an audio snapshot of regional speech in Britain in 2005. And that is exactly what happened.

Such a project had never been undertaken before. If only it had been. I think many people would love to have an audio record of how people spoke regionally in earlier decades. How did people sound around the country in the 1920s, the 1930s...? Those voices have gone for ever now. All we have are fragments that happened to be recorded at the time, as part of one radio programme or another. The quality is often patchy, and many parts of the country have nothing at all. *Voices* 2005 was a huge step forward in recording coverage. I hope they do it again, and again, and again...

Dozens of radio programmes came out of the project, illustrating a great variety of lengths and approaches. Regional speakers of all ages and backgrounds were inter-viewed. It was good to see urban ethnic variation included, as well as the traditionally recognized rural and urban dialects. You don't just get 'Scouse' in Liverpool these days, but Caribbean Scouse, Chinese Scouse, and much more.

Several television programmes were made. This was an interesting development, as it killed stone dead the old idea—which I was often told by television executives in the 1970s—that 'you can't film language'. Language is people, so you film them. One programme, *Word on the Street*, was made in Leicestershire, and looked at how accent and dialect changed from one generation of a family to the next, from grandparents to grandchildren. Another took the form of an accent tour of English in Wales, *The Way We Say It*.

I was involved in both of them, and for the programme about Wales found myself—for the first time in my life—a television co-presenter. The project took quite some time, because we visited over a dozen locations and interviewed people from all walks of life; but it was well worth it. I met sheep-farmers and bingo-callers, market traders and fairground-men, miners and rugby players, social workers and shop assistants. The result was a fascinating insight into the extraordinary range of accents to be found in modern Wales and the strongly held—and very positive—attitudes of the people who used them.

People sometimes say that linguistics is dull. Dull? Driving around Wales in a Porsche in the company of Jane Harvey, one of television's most charming presenters? It is the stuff of 65-year-old fantasies. Do linguistics, I say, and see the world! After the programme, my image rose enormously in my home town.

People also say that accents and dialects are dying out. *Voices Week* showed that they are not. They are alive and well, all over the country. They are changing, of course. Some of the old rural dialects are disappearing, as the way of life changes, and many people are sad about that. But they are being replaced by a range of new dialects, reflecting modern living patterns and a multicultural society.

Voices was a BBC project. And something significant happens when a national organization such as the BBC takes a stand on language matters. The linguistic climate changes. It is not something individuals can do. Only very occasionally do individuals change national attitudes to language. We saw it happening in the eighteenth century, with such people as Johnson. It may have happened today, with Lynne Truss. But usually our views about language are shaped by much greater forces. The country's institutions.

National institutions have played their part in the usage story since the Middle Ages. The primary institution then was the Court. Later, we saw the influence of Chancery, the Church, the Press, and the Public Schools. The BBC, along with other major broadcasting organizations, such as CNN, is the latest institution to influence usage. Perhaps not the latest. The Internet is probably too young to be called an institution, but it will be one day.

Institutions have enormous linguistic power. They sometimes exercise this influence through individuals—particular monarchs, printers, authors, teachers—but more usually the influence is something which arises out of the cumulative impact of a group of key people using language in the same way. A large number of people unconsciously collaborated in the Middle Ages to produce what eventually became standard English. The Authorized Version of the Bible was the result of a committee. So was much of the early character of BBC English.

It is sometimes possible to trace a specific instance of usage, or of an attitude to a usage, to an institutional source. This is how the prescriptive approach started, as we have seen, through the medium of dictionaries and grammars.

They are institutions too. Individual words and phrases can be traced to an influential text, such as the idioms (*salt of the earth*, *den of thieves*...) which originate in the language of the Bible. Today, we can identify the source of many catch-phrases in the media: *What's up, Doc?* (from Bugs Bunny cartoons), *Say It With Flowers* (from an Interflora ad in 1917), *Doh!* (courtesy of Homer Simpson). The last an institution? Of course the Simpsons are an institution.

You will find several hundred such examples in English. Maybe even a thousand. But not ten thousand. Usages are not usually traceable in this way, because they are affected by many influences acting together. Who knows who first used the high rising intonation at the end of a sentence? Historical linguists have traced it back to somewhere in New Zealand in the 1970s, but it may have appeared more or less simultaneously in other countries. Who knows who first changed the stress from <u>contro</u>versy to con<u>tro</u>versy? Who knows who first used *gay* to mean homosexual?

The *Oxford English Dictionary* is in the business of tracing the history of words. Only very rarely is it possible to find a genuine origin. An example is *blurb*, for the publisher's statement on the back of a book, which we know was invented by US humorist Gelett Burgess in 1907. But most new words and new meanings arrive without anyone knowing (or caring) where they came from. Even when the big guns of television are added to those of lexicography, as happened with the BBC2 series *Balderdash and Piffle* in 2006, we are unlikely to trace the history of a word back to its origin. We can push back our understanding of how words were used by a few years or even decades. But origins remain elusive.

The BBC is a great institution. So is the *Oxford English Dictionary*. But there is one institution which, in terms of its influence on the way we use language, is greater than all other institutions combined. It is the school.

28

Education

Wʜᴀᴛ happens to us in school shapes our linguistic preferences and intuitions in a way that nothing else can. When the schools change their linguistic ways, everything changes. It takes a generation or two for the effects to be felt universally. But eventually, everything changes. The first literary quotation in this book was from a schoolteacher, Ælfric (Chapter 1), and so will the last one be.

The eighteenth-century prescriptivists would have got nowhere if the schools hadn't taken up their recommendations and instilled them—often painfully—into the minds of their charges. By the turn of the century, Johnson and Murray ruled in classrooms everywhere. And 'ruled' is not an overstatement.

Nor is 'painful'. When I presented a programme on split infinitives on Radio 4 in the 1980s, I got this letter from a listener:

> The reason why the older generation feel so strongly about English grammar is that we were severely punished if we didn't obey the rules! One split infinitive, one whack; two split infinitives, two whacks; and so on.

He would have been punished for saying *The reason why* too. That was another usage which was frowned upon.

The novelists saw what was going on, and—having been through it—poked fun at it. Here is George Eliot in *Middlemarch*:

> Mrs Garth, like most celebrated educators, had her favourite ancient paths, and in a general wreck of society would have tried to hold her 'Lindley Murray' above the waves.

And here is one of many nods in the direction of school grammar by Charles Dickens, this one—from *Nicholas Nickleby*—gathering together a host of allusions in one glorious piece of characterization:

> 'Is that you?' inquired Peg. 'Ah! It's me, and me's the first person singular, nominative case, agreeing with the verb "it's", and governed by Squeers understood, as a acorn, a hour; but when the h is sounded, the a only is to be used, as a and, a art, a ighway,' replied Mr Squeers, quoting at random from the grammar. 'At least, if it isn't, you don't know any better. And if it is, I've done it accidentally.'

Wackford Squeers was all heart. When one of the boys died, he did the best he could for him:

> A candle in his bed-room on the very night he died—the best dictionary sent up for him to lay his head upon.

It was the school system which eventually made standard English a social reality. It had succeeded in doing so for Latin, and it had the same impact on English. Children were drilled in every detail. They worked their way steadily through the long lists in spelling books. They parsed their way through every side road in English grammar. Here is Dickens again, this time reporting a conversation between a schoolteacher, Miss Peecher, and her favourite pupil, Mary Anne, who now helps her in her household. Mary Anne has just made a comment about a lady: 'They say she's very handsome,' and this triggers a response:

'Oh, Mary Anne, Mary Anne... how often have I told you not to use that vague expression, not to speak it in that general way? When you say *they say*, what do you mean? Part of speech, They?'

Mary Anne hooked her right arm behind her in her left hand, as being under examination, and replied:

'Personal pronoun.'

'Person, They?'

'Third person.'

'Number, They?'

'Plural number.'

'Then how many do you mean, Mary Anne? Two? Or more?

Mary Anne begs Miss Peecher's pardon, as she had meant only one.

Inevitably, it was this same school system which made non-standard English, as defined by the prescriptive grammarians, a social reality too. Doubtless many children then—as in the twentieth century—came to school speaking naturally and colloquially, only to have the proscribed features beaten out of them. Mary Anne, please leave your end-placed prepositions in the gutter, where they belong!

Yes, this system lasted until the middle of the twentieth century. That was just 200 years—from the decade which saw the publication of Johnson and Lowth (1755–65) to the decade which saw their legacy disappear from the curriculum. It was not surprising that it lasted so long. As I said earlier, language does not exist in a vacuum. It receives its status and its form through a social agreement. As long as there was a sharply defined class-based power structure in English-speaking society, there would be a sharply defined linguistic system to represent it. U and Non-U. And this would be taught in schools.

Once the social system started to change, it was only a matter of time before its language, and its associated language teaching, would change. In fact, the schools were in some respects ahead of the game. One of the most significant signs of social change was the movement for political independence, which really gained momentum in the early 1960s, when twenty African countries achieved nationhood. The 1950s and 1960s also saw the arrival in the UK of a large immigrant population, whose speech introduced a new ethnic dimension to British dialectology. But by then, the old-style language teaching had largely disappeared. When Lynne Truss went to grammar school in 1966, it had already gone.

The 1950s. The last classes of children who went through the old system—who were taught about split infinitives and all the other prescriptive rules, and who passed their English language examinations by being able to spot them and mark them wrong—are in their sixties now. They are still influential, as many of them are now in very senior positions in society. But it does not take a crystal ball to see that their time is almost over.

I alluded in my Preface to generations of prescriptivists eating, shooting, and leaving. It is only a rhetorical trope, but I enjoy the wordplay, so bear with me. The trope applies especially to the present generation, who were force-fed the prescriptive legacy to the point where they thought it was good for them. Many, in the manner of Stockholm syndrome, bonded with their captors and became neo-prescriptivists. They then spent much of their lives exploding at regular intervals when they observed later generations failing to observe the rules they had painfully learned. And they are about to leave the scene—I hope not *just* yet, for I am one of their generation. But leave they must.

I often wonder: Why didn't I become a prescriptivist? I learned all those rules. I had to pass all my English language exams. I was beaten as much as they were. Why did *I* not go down their road?

It must have been something to do with the linguistic environment in which I was brought up. I was reared in a bilingual community, in Holyhead in north Wales, where several accents and languages (including Latin and Irish) surrounded me. We travelled to Ireland a lot too, where my mother's family lived.

Then at 11 I found myself in Liverpool, where I did my secondary schooling, and my Welsh accent was immediately beaten out of me. But, unbeknown to my assailants, it was really only beaten a bit deeper into me, for I was able to switch back into it with ease when my family went back on holiday to Wales. I was childishly bilingual at 10 and seriously bidialectal at 11. The concept that there was just one kind of English worth talking made no sense to me. I needed my Welsh linguistic identity to survive in Wales, my Scouse one to survive in Liverpool, and my Irish one to feel at home in Ireland.

I was already—as literary critic George Steiner would later put it—extraterritorial. And I think anyone who has had to move around like this, acquiring fresh linguistic identities, is likely to become more broad-minded when it comes to usage. Certainly, when I arrived at University College London in 1959 and found myself being told about linguistic change and variation, it all seemed as natural as breathing. I must have been a cradle linguist. I never had a moment of conversion, as did St Paul, along a dusty road.

Climates

S o why did old-style grammar disappear in the 1960s? And what took its place? The reasons are many and various.

The decline in grammar teaching didn't start in that decade. Criticisms of traditional grammar were already growing among educationists in the early part of the twentieth century. Teachers found the old approach complex and unrewarding. They didn't like the use of terms (such as *nominative* and *accusative*) which suited Latin grammar but not English. They didn't like the rigid and complicated system of parsing. They didn't like the way the prescriptive approach focused on idiosyncrasies instead of on the broad picture. They didn't like the use of concocted examples rather than real usage. The list of objections goes on and on.

On the other hand, what were they to put in its place? Hardly any academic research was taking place into grammar in the early decades of the century in Britain. And the academic work which *was* being done—the historical study of the language, or *philology*—was considered to be irrelevant to children whose primary need was literacy. Philology was particularly repugnant to teachers of English literature, who found it a dry and dusty subject. And literature teachers in any case were naturally reluctant to give up some of their precious teaching time to the study of a subject whose value had not yet been demonstrated.

Even those who were trying to find a place for grammar teaching were confused. There is a sad comment in a report from a 1921 Board of Education committee: it is, they say,

> impossible at the present juncture to teach English grammar in the schools for the simple reason that no-one knows exactly what it is.

We can see why. There were no academic specialists to advise; and the teachers themselves lacked experience. Grammar had not been compulsory in primary schools since 1890, and the secondary schools were doing little more than recycling old material, which sometimes dated back to Lindley Murray. Fresh initiatives were lacking. The subject was still being taught, but without any life. Grammar had become an academic zombie.

The basic problem was that there was no means of relating the analytical skills involved in doing grammar to the practical skills involved in speaking, listening, reading, and writing. The grammarians argued that there just *had* to be a connection—that any child who learned to parse would inevitably end up being a better user of its language. But there was nothing at all inevitable about it. And there was an obvious counter-argument, best summed up in an analogy. I have a friend who is a wonderful car mechanic—but he is a terrible driver.

The analogy is worth developing. To be a good driver takes a lot more than knowledge of how a car engine works. All kinds of fresh sensitivities and awarenesses are involved. Indeed, most of us learned to drive with next to no understanding of what goes on inside the bonnet. It is the same with language. As we shall see in the next chapter, something else has to happen if children are to use a knowledge of grammar in order to become better speakers, listeners, readers, or writers. A connection has to be made—and, more to the point, demonstrated.

But it is not possible to make a connection if people do not know what is being connected. And neither of the two 'ends' were in a satisfactory state, during the early decades of the century. At the 'engine' end, there was only the seriously deficient system of prescriptive grammar. At the 'driving' end, there were no fresh descriptions of what was involved in the tasks of speaking, listening, reading, and writing, because the research wasn't being done. To continue the analogy, before it dies howling, students were being given a car with most of the bits missing or faulty, and were being asked to drive it without being trained in any highway code or given road maps or tourist guides to show them where they might go. As the English Association put it, with remarkable understatement, in 1923: the teaching of grammar was a 'vexed question'.

By the 1950s, the grammar movement had, quite simply, run out of steam—or perhaps I should say petrol. Grammar was steadily being squeezed out of the syllabus by literature. Teacher-training courses were cutting down on it.

The university English departments were showing little interest in it. There was indeed a new and potentially relevant subject, linguistics, which studied grammar; but most linguists were preoccupied with language and languages in general rather than with English in particular. There was plenty of grammatical activity in Europe. Indeed, all the major English grammars from those years were written by scholars from the Continent, such as Jespersen, Kruisinga, and Zandvoort. And in the USA, Charles Fries was one of a few linguists who valiantly worked away at making a connection. But he had no counterpart in the UK.

If anything was a kiss of death, it was the Secondary Schools Examination Council report of 1964, known as the Lockwood Report. Paragraph 51 contains one of its most devastating criticisms. It is worth quoting in full:

> Our eighth criticism is directed to that part of the present papers which consists of questions on grammatical and other minutiae. Some of the most eloquently critical replies we received from the schools were directed against these questions; we share the view that they are of doubtful utility in any examination of English language and that in their present form they do great harm. Such questions are often based on a few usages which are appropriate enough in some styles of language, but which have come to be traditionally condemned as incorrect in all. Other exercises in the same class are based on traditionally prescribed rules of grammar which have been artificially imposed upon the language. They have had little relevance to usage at any past time and they have even less to contemporary usage. No examination is serving a useful

purpose for schools, candidates, employers or the outside world generally if it encourages pupils to adopt a form of examination room English instead of seeking to express appropriately what they have to say.

And so, one day, the teaching of grammar in Britain quietly died. It is difficult to assign a precise date. It varied somewhat between examining boards and schools. Some schools kept the subject going for a few years, but most dropped it. If I had to choose a year for a tombstone, I would choose the year that the grammar and usage questions were finally dropped by the Ordinary Level (O-level) and Certificate of Secondary Education (CSE) Boards: 1965.

I noticed the change a decade later, when students who had gone through secondary school without any grammar training began to come through to the universities. In my first-year lectures I would always use some examples from prescriptive grammar. 'You will of course all know about not ending sentences with a preposition,' I would say, and the class would nod, already bored. But one year I said this, and instead of nodding bored assent the class shook heads in puzzlement. 'What is the problem?' I asked. 'Please, what's a preposition?' asked one. 'How many of you don't know what a preposition is?' I asked. Well over half put their hands up.

One girl tentatively raised her hand. 'I think I know', she said. I nodded encouragement. 'Is it something to do with getting on a horse?' She saw my horrified face, and hastily added. 'I was taught there was a pre-position before mounting, you see.'

So that is the answer to the third question with which I opened this chapter. What was grammar teaching replaced by? Nothing.

It was such a shame, because by the mid-1960s the linguists had begun to get their act together. Randolph Quirk had started his huge Survey of English Usage in 1960. This was a completely fresh attempt to describe the grammar of all the major varieties of spoken and written British English, compiling a large collection (a 'corpus') of real samples of usage. I worked on the Survey for a while, in 1962–3. It was a wonderfully exciting project. In due course, the research produced a series of major grammars, including the magisterial *A Comprehensive Grammar of the English Language* in 1985. And the corpus approach continues to play a major role in linguistics today.

All this work had one important effect. By the time the climate had begun to change once again, with people beginning to think that grammar wasn't such a bad thing after all, a huge amount of information had been amassed about what English grammar was like. No board of education could have said, in the 1980s, that 'we do not know exactly what it is'. We knew, right down to the last brass adjective.

Why did the linguistic climate change? A mixture of things. There was a dawning realization that the baby had been thrown out with the bathwater. A number of educational language projects had been planned by linguists and teachers working in collaboration. Fresh materials had been written. Teachers began to explore with their students the different domains of 'language in use'—the language of advertising, religion, science, law, sports commentary... But they quickly encountered a problem: they had no terminology to talk about what they encountered in these domains. How could they teach their students to describe the interesting ways in which an advertiser used adjectives if the students had no idea what an adjective was? Let alone a preposition.

At the same time, the new ideas about grammar were beginning to reach a wider public. The differences between spoken and written English were being unravelled. A new relationship was emerging between language and literature, thanks to developments in stylistics. Growing multiculturalism demanded greater respect for the grammatical features of ethnic dialects. Fresh perspectives emerged as people explored grammar from novel points of view, such as how children acquired sentence structure. The message from foreign-language teachers, speech therapists, teachers of the deaf, and many other professionals was plain. Grammar is useful, if it's taught properly. It was a big *if*, but a consensus grew that it was time to explore new ways of getting it back into the mainstream curriculum. The English committees—Bullock, Kingman, Cox—set to work.

I was one of several linguists who spent dozens of days each year, during those formative decades, putting the case for more systematic English language study to groups of interested professionals. Some of the best days were with the English inspectorate, whose in-service conferences at the Abbey Hotel in Malvern produced some of the most stimulating interactions I have ever encountered. Other days were with the teachers themselves, at all levels. There was real interest. People wanted the baby back—but not the prescriptive bathwater. And eventually the baby was born. They called it the National Curriculum for English.

Whatever the limitations of this Curriculum, it does two things superbly well. First, it introduces a balance between the study of language structure and the study of language use. It avoids the failings of traditional grammar because it insists that any focus on a bit of language should be accompanied by an awareness of how that bit of language is used in real life. And it avoids the failings of the 'language in use' movement of the 1970s because it insists that any study of a linguistic domain (such as advertising) should be accompanied by an awareness of the bits of language needed to express it. This balance, between structure and use, is a first, in English linguistic history.

And the Curriculum has managed to pull together many of the trends towards a comprehensive and realistic language awareness that I have been discussing throughout this book. It has totally rejected the prescriptive mentality. Standard English continues to be seen as a major educational goal, but it is viewed in an inclusive way, with all varieties—spoken and written, formal and informal, professional and everyday—taken into account. Literacy remains the centre of attention, especially at primary school level. And grammar is put in its place, alongside vocabulary, pronunciation, orthography, and the structure of discourse. That is why I talked about 'bits of language' above. There is much more to language than grammar.

None of this, though, is at the expense of non-standard English. Regional and ethnic accents and dialects, national and international, in general use and in literature, are studied with equal respect, and students explore their function as expressions of regional and social identity. The relationship between standard and non-standard usage is carefully investigated. It is not—it never has been—a matter of 'anything goes'. This is the kind of silly remark that prescriptively minded people make when they can think of nothing better to say. On the contrary: the whole point is to get across to students the notion that 'anything' *doesn't* 'go'. The principle of appropriateness rules.

As an educational language policy, the new Curriculum is in my view second to none, and the direction of thinking has been influential in other English-speaking countries. But is it working?

30

Future

AT the outset, it was difficult to see how the new English National Curriculum could ever work. Here was a splendid teaching model being introduced into schools—but there were few teachers trained or experienced enough to teach it, and there were few textbooks or other materials available to illustrate it. Older teachers, meanwhile, realizing that 'grammar was back', rummaged around for their ancient grammar books, thinking that this was where they came in. The National Literacy Strategy, introduced in 1999, struggled to come to terms with terminology.

It was a tricky time. I well remember working overtime during the 1990s doing in-service courses on grammar to group after group of teachers. The Advanced-level syllabuses in English language were also in place, and they were proving unexpectedly popular. Some boards noted that more students were studying English language at A-level than English literature. Once every few weeks, I found myself working with John Shuttleworth, one of the A-level examiners, exploring the best ways in which grammar could be shown to help improve skills in those four central domains—speaking, listening, reading, and writing. It wasn't difficult to do, once the right approach had been found.

This isn't the place to go into detail; I have done that in my *Making Sense of Grammar* and other books. But I can reiterate the crucial principle: grammar must never be left to its own devices. The main purpose of grammar, as I said in Chapter 15, is to enable us to make sense. The examples there showed that vocabulary alone is not enough. But grammar is not enough either. It is the collaboration between these two domains which facilitates our expression and comprehension. Or, putting this another way, grammar must never be taught without studying the meanings that the various words and constructions express. As linguists would say: grammar needs the foundation of semantics, if it is to succeed in explaining how we communicate with each other. When things go wrong, and we become unclear or ambiguous, we need to study both the words and the structures to work out what happened.

But there is more. It is not enough just to study the words and structures. Sentences have to be put to use, and that very operation requires that we study the contexts in which they appear. The demands made upon our sentences in the context of science are very different from those made in the context of everyday conversation. Think now of all the possible demands that contexts make upon us. Lawyers, priests, sports commentators, advertisers, politicians, newsreaders, journalists, civil servants, emailers, website designers… all use language in their individual ways, with varying effectiveness. We know that we need to change our language—as we do our clothes (Chapter 16)—as we move from one context to another. And there are hundreds of contexts.

This is where things start to get really interesting, and where, finally, the kind of approach I am advocating in this book links up with the issues that disturb such writers as John Humphrys (Chapter 23). The examples of 'meaningless drivel' which cause him such pain, from contexts as different as politics and advertising, need careful analysis, if we are to expose them for what they are—or, alternatively, discover that they are not as meaningless as we had expected. This means examining all aspects of their language in a systematic way. And it is what present-day students are being trained to do.

Walk into an A-level English language class these days—or, for that matter, lower down the school, into classes where teachers have engaged successfully with the focus on grammar in the National Literacy Strategy—and you would see some fine examples of this approach in practice. You would see students looking critically at the words people use, the sentences in which they use them, the way in which the sentences are put to work in discourse, and whether these discourses suit the context in which the speakers or writers are operating. In short, they are learning to judge appropriateness in others.

At the same time, the students are being trained to use the same kind of analysis in relation to their own self-expression. They need to discover which words, sentences, and patterns of discourse best suit the purposes they themselves have in mind. They need to see what happens when they change from one word or grammatical construction to another—not just in terms of the change of meaning, but in terms of the impact the change has on their audience. In short, they are learning to judge appropriateness in themselves.

We can sum it up in another way: students are being taught to recognize and understand the consequences of making linguistic *choices*. Every sentence we speak or write involves a choice. We hope we have made the right choices—that we have chosen language which is both meaningful and acceptable to our listeners and readers. Sometimes we get it only half right. We say something meaningful but it is phrased in an unacceptable way. Or we speak in an acceptable style, but not very clearly. Ideally, we should try to satisfy both criteria, and be in a position to judge if other people have satisfactorily achieved them.

In a nutshell: we need to know what we are doing. We need to be in control of our language, and not have it control us. As Lewis Carroll's Humpty Dumpty once said, referring to the way he changed word meanings at will: 'the question is: which is to be master—that's all.' We have to be masters of language.

None of this can be done in a day or two, any more than mastery of a work of literature or a complex chemical formula can be fully appreciated in a day or two. It takes years to build up the necessary skills. And that is why the National Curriculum stresses the importance of working to develop a child's sense of linguistic appropriateness from the very beginning of schooling. The examples of usage at an early age will be very different, of course. But it is just as possible to have a junior class talk interestingly about the language of cartoon characters and nursery rhymes as it is to have a senior class talk about that of editorials and political speeches.

It is a great vision, and we are steadily moving towards its implementation. But there is a long way to go, for it is obvious that there is much still to be done by way of teacher training and the provision of teaching materials. This is one of the criticisms that has often been made of recent educational policy: it was introduced without enough preparatory work being in place. I am still out there, doing in-service courses, and I really shouldn't need to be, fifteen years on. There seems to be no let-up in the demand. It is taking much longer to make the new Curriculum work than its devisers thought.

I am not entirely surprised. It took a generation—by which I mean twenty years or so—for prescriptivism to get into all the schools, and it took a generation to get it out again. It will presumably take a generation to get the new vision thoroughly and universally established. There is already a review process in place to evaluate how we are doing. In February 2005 the Qualifications and Curriculum Authority launched 'English 21', to generate a national discussion about what the teaching of English should be like in 2015.

We are still learning how to develop this inclusive vision of language in society. It has never been done before, so it is difficult to anticipate all the pitfalls. Inclusiveness means what it says. Language is the responsibility of everyone, so everyone must be involved in the outcome. And one of the pitfalls which was early encountered, in implementing the new Curriculum, was that not everyone had been equally involved. In particular, the planners had forgotten about parents.

Teachers can't forget about parents. They are always there in the background, often in the playground. They have views about language too, but—in view of the lack of language work in their own schooldays—they are usually uninformed views. So there is often a clash between parents and teachers who are trying to introduce the new thinking. I remember attending one PTA meeting where the English teachers were being given a hard time by some parents because they thought a particular homework exercise was pointless. The problem? The children had been asked to rewrite a story in the style of a football sports commentary.

It is impossible to explain a new climate of educational linguistic thinking in the charged atmosphere of a PTA meeting. Later, in a smaller meeting, the teachers were able to get the parents to see the point. But they shouldn't have had to do that. Somebody in the Department of Education should have thought to explain what was going on to parents at the outset. This didn't happen. And as a result, a lot of the energy that teachers should have been devoting to developing better classroom practice went into handling unnecessarily worried parents.

There were other distractions. It is a truism, at this point in the book, to say that people easily get upset about usage. But it is easy to forget just how deep-rooted these feelings are, and how quickly they come to the surface. This was another thing that the planners didn't sufficiently anticipate. They forgot that teachers have feelings too.

I remember being part of an in-service training day for English teachers. The oldest members of the group were in their fifties; the youngest were in their twenties. The talk was about usage, and it soon became apparent that there was a world of difference between the generations. The older members had been trained in old-style grammar. The younger ones had no formal language training at all. An argument began over whether it was right to teach children to put a comma before *and* in such phrases as *tall, dark and handsome* (Chapter 21). Emotions rose. I remember the closing remark, before the meeting broke up in disarray. One member shouted at another: 'That's exactly the kind of stupid thing I'd expect to hear from someone who wears a yellow tie with spots on it!' We all went for coffee.

Sadly, that is all too typical. Arguments about language often segue into arguments about behaviour in general. There is no necessary connection between language and intelligence, language and criminal behaviour, or—heaven help us—language and yellow spotted ties; but people readily assume there is. These feelings all have to be brought out into the open and discussed. They are there, lurking in every English department. A school has to evolve a language policy in which differences of opinion about usage are managed. Otherwise the children suffer. One teacher corrects the comma; the other doesn't. Stand by for the next PTA meeting.

When educationists develop a language policy, they need to think carefully about the feelings of the people who have to implement it and live with it—which chiefly means the teachers and the parents. Very little of this kind of thinking seems to have been done. The focus has almost entirely been on the needs of the students. That is all well and good, but if the feelings of the other participants in the educational process are insufficiently considered, the task of meeting student needs is made much more difficult than it needs to be.

And there is one other group I must not forget at this point, for their spirit is present on every page of this book. These are the pundits, the pedants, the purists, the watchdogs, the Trussians, the letter-writers to Radio 4, the people who—as John Humphrys does—care passionately about the language. They may be speaking as individuals or as members of groups—such as the Queen's English Society, the Plain English Campaign, or the Society for the Protection of the Apostrophe. But they have feelings—very strong feelings, usually—and these have to find a place in a language policy too.

Their role is important, because they define one end of the tolerance spectrum. Students need to know that there is a 'zero tolerance' position with respect to usage, because it helps them to place themselves in relation to it. If teachers are inculcating attitudes of respect towards language use, then, even if they disagree totally with zero tolerance, they need to treat it dispassionately. Condemning purism out of hand is as useless as condemning its opposite. Students need to know about pedants. Pedants have their place. After all, without them, there would be no way of teaching young people how not to be pedantic.

I'm joking, I'm joking. As I said earlier, the language pundits play an important role in alerting us to the ways in which difficulties can be caused by language change. Change can't be stopped, but it does need to be managed. They also provide a critical perspective for uses of language where the users have let everyone down by genuine examples of laziness, carelessness, lack of training, lack of thought, or a deliberate attempt to obfuscate. These are not appropriate or acceptable behaviours. They break my basic principle (Chapter 16).

I too get irate when a broadcaster gabbles and makes it difficult to understand what he or she is saying. I too worry about what politicians are up to when they speak evasively. I am as much against obscure English in public documents as anyone. I applaud the motives of the Plain English Campaign, and its US sister, and have sometimes worked with them. They even call their accolade a Crystal Mark— though not, I have to say, with me in mind when they named it.

I actually value linguistic pedantry. It has its place in a complete picture of language in society. But we must remember that there are pedants and pedants. I would not want to group together the intelligent and good-humoured pedantry of Lynne Truss and John Humphrys with those who regularly send me hate mail because I see nothing wrong in split infinitives. I am quite used to being rudely told off by members of purist societies. If I had a pound for every time my work has been dismissed as totally irrelevant to the real issues of the day...

I am usually described by pedants as 'one of those permissives', an 'anything goes' man. One of the reasons for writing this book is to nail this myth once and for all. So Read My Lips. I have never, never said that 'anything goes' when it comes to usage. Nor has any other linguist. The principle of appropriateness goes clean against such a silly position. If pedants really knew about the way linguists look at language, they would see the absurdity straight away. At the heart of linguistics is the distinction between 'grammatical' and 'ungrammatical', between 'acceptable' and 'unacceptable'. It is the boundary line which attracts all the arguments. And that is only a tiny part of the story of usage.

Nailing the myth? I should be so lucky. 'Anything goes' is an easy term of abuse. So I expect people who disagree with me will carry on doing so—unless this book has happened to persuade them that my position is not as irrational as they thought it was. Maybe my attempt to explain the history of English usage will convince them that the situation is not as bad as they believed, that the language is not going down the drain, that there is value in language change, and that there is richness in language variation. Or maybe not.

Comments about usage began a thousand years ago. Abbot Ælfric would have been proud of today's students. We don't care what we talk about, said his charges, 'as long as the speech is correct': 'buton hit riht spræc sy'. I translated *riht* as 'correct' in Chapter 1. I would translate it as 'appropriate' now. Otherwise—apart from the beatings— the comment still applies. And the next generation of students will be in a better position to distinguish linguistic sense from nonsense than any previous generation since English began.

I wrote this book to explain why English usage became such an issue—why, in short, so many millions bought *Eats, Shoots and Leaves*. I'm still not sure I understand, entirely, why punctuation attracted such special interest or what the purchasers were (are) expecting that book to do. But I do think I know why people feel so insecure about their language, and why the issue is rumbling on, and that is what I have tried to focus on in *The Fight for English*. It has been a battle, indeed. A battle lasting half a millennium. I think it is drawing to its close now. I hope so.

Epilogue

I am mentioned on the penultimate page of John Humphrys' book *Lost for Words*. He gives me a sympathetic assessment, for which I am grateful. But I still find myself labelled there as 'very much an "anything goes" man'.

Cut now to an early morning late in 2005. I am on *Today*. Apparently, the previous day John had been interviewing an author of a book about English social history. 'What's the book about?', the author was asked. And the reply was couched entirely in a tense form that grammarians call the 'historic present'. Instead of saying

> People were concerned about housing. They wanted more jobs...

the author said

> People are concerned about housing. They want more jobs...

and he went on like this until John, hopelessly confused, intervened. Was the author talking about then or now? He couldn't work it out.

I don't have a recording of the interview, so these are not so much quotations as memories. But they capture the point. Here was somebody talking about the nineteenth century as if it were 2005. The same social issues turned up then as now. No wonder John was confused. The hapless historian got a good telling-off for his use of the historic present.

If the author had read *Lost for Words*, he might have avoided getting into trouble. There we are told that it is not one of John's favourite constructions. Using the historic present to John Humphrys in the early morning must be the linguistic equivalent of holding a red rag up to a bull.

The email-bag that day was full. Lots of listeners apparently wrote in sharing his dislike of the usage. The producers sensed an Issue. So the next day I was asked to comment.

I don't know what they were expecting. Perhaps, they hoped, a 'lively discussion' (as the euphemism goes) would ensue, with Professor Anything Goes doubtless saying there was nothing at all wrong with it and being beaten up as a consequence. If so, they got a shock.

Of course there was something wrong with it, and that is what I said. It was inept behaviour on the part of the author. The historic present only works if it is clear from the linguistic context what the time-frame is. Take the second sentence of the second paragraph of this Epilogue. Did you even notice that it was in the historic present? I could have written 'I was on *Today*', but I felt the present tense made the story-telling more dramatic. That is what this tense form does. It dramatizes.

There was no ambiguity, however. This is because the preceding sentence made it clear that the time of reference was 2005. It is now 2006—or whenever you are reading this. You know it cannot be 2005. In any case, you know I cannot be on *Today* if I am writing a book. So there is no chance of any ambiguity.

But you cannot do this sort of thing on the radio and get away with it, without being very careful. It's all right to start off by saying

> Conditions in 1850 were very bad. Imagine. People are often ill...

But half a minute later we have forgotten that crucial bit of opening context. We have lost the track. If the speaker is using the present tense, the sentences seem to be referring to present time—that is, now. And apart from anything else, any listener who tuned in after the opening sentence about 1850 would be totally lost.

To make the historic present work, on the radio, you have to keep reminding listeners that the context is set in the past. This is easy enough with an account where the names of characters and the historical setting is enough to maintain the sense:

> Henry VIII orders the destruction of the monasteries... As a result of the Dissolution he acquires huge amounts of gold and silver plate...

But it is very hard when the topic is one that could equally well apply today. You have to keep adding context:

> People are concerned about housing in the nineteenth century. They want more jobs...

The style quickly becomes wordy, cumbersome, and repetitive. It's bad radio. Our historian author did not fall into that trap. But he messed up his radio opportunity by falling into the other.

He should have told the whole story in the past tense. He would then have had no hassle. John Humphrys would have had no raised blood pressure. And I would have had no Epilogue.

Notes

*These notes give the sources of quotations unless they are already
mentioned in the text.*

PROLOGUE
hoax: *New Yorker*, 28 June 2004.
Sunday Times, 19 February 2006.

CHAPTER I
Ælfric's Colloquy, edited by G. N. Garmonsway (London: Methuen,
   1939).
Lord's Prayer variants: in David Crystal, *The Stories of English*
   (London: Penguin, 2004), p. 45 [referred to below as *Stories*].

CHAPTER 2
Robert of Gloucester: in *Stories*, pp. 128–9.
John of Trevisa: in *Stories*, pp. 129–30.
Chaucer quotations from the complete works edited by
   F. N. Robinson (London: Oxford University Press, 1957).
The Manciple's Tale, l. 205.
The Merchant's Tale, l. 1567.
The Shipman, epilogue to *The Man of Law's Tale*, l. 1188.
The House of Fame, l. 865.
Higden: *Polychronicon*, ch. 59: in *Stories*, pp. 130–1.

CHAPTER 3
Caxton: in N. F. Blake, *Caxton's Own Prose* (London: Deutsch, 1973),
   nos. 36, 50.

Chaucer: in *Stories*, p. 184.
Troilus and Criseyde, l. 1793.

CHAPTER 4

Historical linguistics research into standard English: reviewed in
Stories, chapter 10.

CHAPTER 6

More: 'The Confutacion of Tyndale's Aunswere, made from
Anno 1532', in W. W. Skeat, *Specimens of English Literature*, vol. iii
(Oxford: Oxford University Press, 1886), p. 192.

Tyndale: in A. W. Pollard, *Records of the English Bible* (Oxford:
Oxford University Press, 1911), p. 94.

Boorde: *The Fyrste Boke of the Introduction of Knowledge*, c.1550.

Skelton: *The Boke of Phyllyp Sparowe*, 1545, l. 777.

Elyot: *The Boke Named The Gouernour*, 1531.

Pettie: preface to *The Ciuile Conuersation of M. Steeuen Guazzo*, 1581.

Orwell: 'Politics and the English Language', *Horizon*, 13 (1946).

CHAPTER 7

Sidney: *Defence of Poesie*, 1595.

Camden: *Remaines Concerning Britain*, 1605.

Carew: *The Excellencie of the English Tongue*, 1614.

Wordsworth: 'We must be free or die, who speak the tongue / That
Shakespeare spake' ('England', 1802).

Puttenham: *The Arte of Poesie*, 1589, Book 3 'Of Ornament' and
Book 4 'Of Language'.

Harrison: *Description of Britaine*, 1587.

CHAPTER 8

Chaucer: *The Reeve's Tale*, ll. 4037, 4080.

Notes

CHAPTER 10

Sprat: *A History of the Royal Society of London*, 1667, section 20.

Slack: 'A Divided Society', in Christopher Haigh (ed.), *The Cambridge Historical Encyclopedia of Great Britain and Ireland* (Cambridge: Cambridge University Press, 1985), p. 181.

Dryden: 'In Defence of the Epilogue', reprinted in W. F. Bolton, *The English Language: Essays by English and American Men of Letters 1490–1839* (Cambridge: Cambridge University Press, 1966–9), pp. 55–69 [referred to below as Bolton].

CHAPTER 11

Johnson: 'Preface to Roscommon', in *Prefaces, Biographical and Critical to the Works of the English Poets*, vol. vi, 1779.

Defoe: 'Of Academies', from *An Essay upon Projects*, reprinted in Bolton, pp. 91–101.

Swift: 'A Proposal for Correcting, Improving and Ascertaining the English Tongue', reprinted in Bolton, pp. 107–23.

CHAPTER 12

Chesterfield: *Letters of Lord Chesterfield to his Son* (London: Dent, 1929; Everyman's Library, vol. 823) [referred to below as *Letters*].

CHAPTER 13

Murray: *Grammar*, 5th edition, i.174.

Swift: in Bolton, pp. 107–23.

CHAPTER 14

Johnson: *Rambler*, 14 March 1752, p. 208.

Boswell: *Life of Samuel Johnson* (chapter 20), Thursday, 19 October 1769.

CHAPTER 15

Trifler, 10 (1788), p. 126.

By one count, there are roughly 3,500 points of grammar indexed in Randolph Quirk et al., *The Comprehensive Grammar of the English Language* (London: Longman, 1985).

CHAPTER 17
Murray: *Grammar*, Rule XVII, point 1.

CHAPTER 18
Murray on 'strength': *Grammar*, appendix, chapter 3, fifth rule.
Murray's use of *attended to*: *Grammar*, appendix, chapter 3, seventh rule.
Pictures of the *will/shall* headlines: David Crystal, *The English Language* (London: Penguin, 1988), p. 24.
De Quincy: *Blackwood's Magazine*, April 1839.
The Athenaeum, 23 January 1869, p. 128.

CHAPTER 20
Review by Louis Menand: *New Yorker*, 28 June 2004.
Truss on apostrophes: *Eats, Shoots and Leaves* (London: Profile Books, 2003), p. 15.

CHAPTER 21
Shaw: *The Author*, April 1902.
Murray: *Grammar*, introduction to 'Punctuation'.

CHAPTER 22
Milne: *Winnie-the-Pooh* (London: Methuen, 1926).

CHAPTER 23
Humphrys on dangling participles: *Lost for Words: The Mangling and Manipulating of the English Language* (London: Hodder, 2004), pp. 78–9 [referred to below as Humphrys]
Humphrys on power of expression: p. 50.

Notes

CHAPTER 24

Chesterfield: *Letters*, 19 November 1750.

Webster, first quotation: *Sketches of American Policy*, 1785.

Webster, second quotation: *Dissertations on the English Language*, 1789.

CHAPTER 25

Johnson: preface to the *Dictionary*, 1755.

Murray: *Grammar*, part I, chapter 1, section 2, under N.

Elyot: *The Boke named The Gouernour*, 1531, chapter 5.

Walker: preface to *A Critical Pronouncing Dictionary*.

CHAPTER 26

Lloyd: 'Standard English', *Die Neueren Sprachen*, 2 (1894), p. 52.

Jones: preface to *English Pronouncing Dictionary* (London: Dent, 1917).

Reith: foreword to A. Lloyd James, *Broadcast English* (London: BBC, 1928).

Pickles: *Between You and Me* (London: Werner Laurie, 1929), pp. 146–7.

CHAPTER 28

Listener on split infinitives: David Crystal, *Who Cares About English Usage* (London: Penguin, 1984), p. 27.

Middlemarch, 1871–2, book III, chapter 24.

Nicholas Nickleby, 1838–9, chapter 57 and chapter 4.

Steiner: *Extraterritorial* (London: Faber and Faber, 1972).

CHAPTER 29

Education history: see R. Hudson and J. Walmsley, 'The English Patient: English Grammar and Teaching in the Twentieth Century', *Journal of Linguistics*, 41 (2005), pp. 593–622.

Board of Education: *The Teaching of English in England* (London: HMSO, 1921, Newbolt Report), p. 291.

English Association: *The Problem of Grammar* (English Association Pamphlet, 56, 1923), p. 3.

EPILOGUE

Humphrys on historic present: pp. 139–40.

Index

Index

Index

-e, pronouncing 30–32
Eats, Shoots and Leaves 226
    a hoax VIII, 137
    a setback 143
    criticized 120
    precedents 108
    related to books on
      manners 79
    selectivity 133, 144
    why a success VII–IX, 218
Edwards, Huw 186
eggs story in Caxton 14–15
Eliot, George 194, 227
Elizabethan literature 43, 60
elocution courses 175
eloquence, negative
  view of 61–4
Elyot, Thomas 38, 171,
  224, 227
encyclopedic names 167–8
English:
    British vs. American
      15, 164–8
    global 22, 166–7
    golden age 43
    good vs. bad 101, 158
    Middle 8–9, 12, 18–27
    Old 3–5, 15, 25–6, 41,
      110, 160
    see also standard English
English Now 182–3, 185
English 21 212
Estuary English 183
etiquette books 78
etymology 29
Evelyn, John 68
explaining language 142–3, 155

expression, expanding
  powers of 160
extraterritorial linguistic
  identity 198

feedback 23–4, 147
formal vs. informal English 112
Fowler brothers 157, 161
French:
    Academy 68, 73
    as model 37
    dislike of 12
    influence on English 7–8
    loan words 7, 13, 41, 117
Fries, Charles 202

g, dropping the 178
Gaelic 11
glossators 4
glottal stops 180
Gower, John 57
Gowers, Ernest 157
grammar:
    as criterion of a standard
      96–7, 110
    change from Old English
      25–6
    first book of 55–6
    in eighteenth century
      94–9
    period of no teaching 155–6,
      196, 199–204
    purpose 96–7
    research 199, 202
    returning in schools 204–7
    writing 4, 124
    see also prescriptive rules

Index

Index

Index

Index